25 Years

By the Big Apple Circus

Foreword

Inside, the tent is midnight blue and speckled with stars. Tiers of seats descend to a red and white circus ring 42 feet in diameter. As you settle into your chair, the smells envelop you: of popcorn, cotton candy and almost 2,000 excited grownups and children. You realize that you can also smell the sawdust inside the ring. Then the lights dim and every hand reaching for popcorn and every mouth chewing cotton candy suddenly stops.

The Big Apple Circus is so close that you can see it, smell it, and almost touch it. Right in front of you, almost in your lap, performers are doing the impossible: Jugglers make balls and clubs dance through the air; horses waltz around the ring in perfect synchronicity; ropewalkers transform a narrow strand of wire into a stroll down a country lane; and perched atop a towering unicycle, itself balancing precariously on a giant rolling globe, a Chinese acrobat nonchalantly kicks one rice bowl after another into the air and somehow catches them on her head. Yet you know that it can not be easy: You see the roped muscles in the back of the smiling aerialist as she glides through the air on the trapeze and the utter concentration of the acrobat about to catch his partner flying head-over-heels. If the circus spirit has caught you and you are game, that clown running through the audience with the gleam in his eyes might...just...pick...you!

At the end of the performance, you leave the Big Apple Circus exhausted — what a show! — yet at the same time refreshed and reinvigorated. For a little less than two hours, all laws of time and space were suspended. No more gravity! People flew, shared space with wild animals (even housecats!), and performed amazing feats of strength and agility. And for real, without special effects or magician's tricks. If they could do that inside the circus tent, surely we could struggle on and even excel in our humdrum daily lives as well.

The American circus was not always like this. For over a century, we thought the circus meant big, bigger, biggest: Parades! Three rings! Tens of thousands in the stands! Performers everywhere you looked! "Get your light sabers here!" Human cannonballs! White elephants! Unicorns! The circus became part of, and even the embodiment of, the great American tradition of ballyhoo and flim-flam. But in doing so, it somehow lost sight of the true essence of circus: People using strength, daring, and artistry to overcome, even for a moment, human limitations.

Then in the early 1970s, a pair of young American juggler-adventurers doing their "grand tour" landed in the single ring of Annie Fratellini's Nouveau Cirque de Paris. For Paul Binder and Michael Christensen, here was something new: one single ring, a sense of warmth and intimacy and sharing with audience, and a level of skill and creativity in the performances that far surpassed anything back in the States. Although it was all novelty to Paul and Michael, they learned that the one-ring circus was actually the true, original circus, not the American version. In fact, the modern circus was born with only one ring back in the late 18th century, and one ring remained the norm all over the world -- everywhere except the United States. And for its audiences, the one-ring circus was not a tired showbiz spectacle but a true popular art form, one that attracted everyone from schoolchildren to the leading artists and intellectuals.

As night after night Paul and Michael performed their juggling routine (involving clubs, a rubber chicken named Leonard, and a lot of patter in bad French), gradually a realization began to dawn: This felt like home. They did not know what they wanted to do with the rest of their lives, but they knew that they wanted to do it around a circus like the Nouveau Cirque de Paris.

In 1976, back in his hometown of New York City between circus seasons, Paul Binder awoke with an idea that rattled his brain like lightning: "The New York School of Circus Arts Presents the Big Apple Circus!" They would re-create in New York City the intimate, classical one ring circus that they had fallen in love with in Paris. New York was undergoing one of its worst fiscal crises ever during that era, but the idea spread like wildfire through a group of visionary artists, circus buffs, civic leaders, and financiers. Out of nothing but that one simple idea, in less than a year they conjured up a traditional 42-foot circus ring and an ill-fitting green tent on a landfill in the shadows of the World Trade Center. On July 18, 1977, the Big Apple Circus held its first performance, writing a new chapter in the history of the American circus. Twenty-five years have now passed. The Big Apple Circus has become one of the world's most celebrated circuses. Performing there is a consecration for circus artists all over the planet, and, indeed, many of the greatest jugglers, aerialists, clowns, acrobats, and animal trainers have graced its single ring. For New Yorkers, their homegrown circus is a much-loved part of the cultural fabric. The Big Apple Circus' 12-week winter season at Manhattan's Lincoln Center has become a holiday tradition, entertaining and amazing everyone from schoolchildren to celebrities. After New York, the circus hits the road, traveling from Boston to Chicago to Atlanta and winning "Ooohs!" and "Aaahs!" and rave reviews wherever it goes. And beyond the circus itself, the Big Apple Circus' four renowned community programs, most notably the Clown Care Unit®, have spread its activity nationwide and inspired similar programs on five continents. This is the story of the Big Apple Circus — Michael and Paul's great adventure — from its difficult beginnings to its latest triumphs. It is also an exhilarating circus family album, filled with treasured memories, photographic and otherwise, from the Big Apple Circus archives, gathered here to celebrate 25 years of pure magic, in and beyond the ring.

Table of Contents

*T*wenty-five years ago, as a small group of artists and riggers, we staked our spirit and our sweat on a remarkable idea: that New York City not only deserved its own tented circus, but would embrace it. We were full of hope, enthusiasm, idealism and energy. It seemed the only thing we weren't full of was patrons in our tent.

Yet, we had faith – not only in New York and its residents, but also in circus. Because, when done well, circus is more than entertainment (but what entertainment it can be!). It's nothing less than a celebration of community, one that touches people's hearts in a way that no other performing art can. We believed that the Big Apple Circus could be a focus of both celebration and service, not just in our metropolitan home, but wherever our travels took us. There was just one question: If we built it, would they come?

They came. You came. Over the past quarter century, the Big Apple Circus has ushered millions of people into our one-ring tent, made friends and found supporters along city streets and rural roads, and led a resurgence of circus across the country.

You came because circus truly is about community. Our focus may be the ring inside a Big Top, but our reach extends far beyond it. Even as our first tent rose along the Hudson River, we began an inner-city circus school that taught teamwork, self-esteem, trust and cooperation. Today its descendant, our Beyond the Ring® program, serves hundreds of kids in public schools around the city. As our summer tour extended to Boston, Atlanta and Chicago, our Clown Care Unit® began reaching out to chronic and acutely ill children. Today the Clown Care Unit makes rounds in 17 hospitals in nine major cities nationwide. Our Circus for All® program distributes circus tickets to 50,000 worthy individuals each season, while Circus of the Senses® performances allow some 10,000 patrons with special needs to experience the magic of the circus.

Here's a book about the first 25 years of the Big Apple Circus, a circus whose heart is as great as the city for which it is named. Both the city and our circus are about great hopes, dreams and, most importantly – community. Is it any wonder we've been around for a quarter of a century?

Paul Binder
Founder and Artistic Director

---

*O*ver 25 years ago, Paul Binder and I walked into our first circus ring, at the Nouveau Cirque de Paris. This was a beautiful French classical one-ring circus founded by Annie Fratellini, a fifth generation circus clown and granddaughter of Paul of the legendary clown trio François, Paul and Albert Fratellini. The finest female circus clown of our generation, Annie passed away in 1997.

After we performed our comedy-juggling act, we would often peek through the curtains and watch Annie and her husband, Pierre Etaix, spin their magic. We became nine-year-olds again, wide-eyed and with mouths agape.

That experience touched a place of childlike wonder in us and was the genesis of the Big Apple Circus. We opened the Big Apple Circus on July 18th, 1977 in Battery Park City, in the shadow of the World Trade Center. On opening night, I walked into the ring to perform and it felt like home. New Yorkers embraced us. And in return, for 25 years, along with the world's finest circus artists, we have put the very best of who we are into our delightful, 42 feet in diameter, sawdust-filled circle of celebration — our home.

They say, "Home is where the heart is." For me, home is also where the magical horse people are, the magical flying people; the magical musical, sound, and light people; the magical throwing-things-into-the-air-and-catching-them-again people, and, of course, the magical fall-down-go-boom-stand-up-again people: the clowns. What a home! Over the years, we've extended that home's living room into New York City schools through our Beyond the Ring Program® as well as into 17 pediatric hospitals across the country through our Big Apple Circus Clown Care Unit®.

As one of those nine-year-old men peeking into Annie Fratellini's magical world, I never dreamed that 25 years later I would be a founding member of a beloved New York institution which shares the joyful spirit of the circus with so many people in so many ways. I am grateful.

Michael Christensen
Co-founder and Creative Director

Paul as Ringmaster, and Michael as 'Mr. Stubs': the final version of their juggling act.(1981)

A Brief History of the Circus

In 1977, Paul Binder and Michael Christensen founded the Big Apple Circus as their way of reviving, in the United States, the great classical tradition of the circus. Their dream was not to "reinvent" the circus, as others would try later. Nor did they want to follow the dominant American model, which then emphasized spectacle and size over artistry. They simply wanted to revive the tradition they discovered when they were invited to perform their juggling act at the Nouveau Cirque de Paris: a one-ring circus, intimate and theatrical, with a focus on artistic excellence.

After Paul's initial inspiration to create a circus for New York City, he visited the New York Public Library for the Performing Arts in order to learn more about circus history. The information he gathered often came as a surprise to him (which is understandable since the history of the circus is little known, even to enthusiasts). Paul's discoveries informed his vision of what a good circus should be and had a strong impact on the subsequent evolution of the Big Apple Circus.

Some of the circus's components are as old as civilization itself. Two thousand years before the Common Era, jugglers, acrobats, and animal trainers appeared as full-fledged entertainers in Egypt in the West and China in the East (where they would eventually create the uniquely Asian "acrobatic theater"). The Egyptians taught the Greeks, and the Greeks taught the Romans, and companies of visual entertainers known as *funambuli* traveled across the vast Roman Empire performing wherever they could, usually in town squares. (The Romans also had their famous "circus," primarily featuring chariot races, but this is in reality the ancestor of the modern racetrack, not of the circus as we know it.)

During the Middle Ages, the traveling performers who were heirs to the funambuli found a perfect setting for their exhibitions of strength and agility in the gigantic commercial fairs that blossomed from London to Vladivostok. They became known as *saltibanchi*, or "mountebanks," literally, "those who jump onto the bank," which was a makeshift stage made of boards laid across a pair of barrels or sawhorses. In these same fairs, money lenders used similar "banks," from behind which they conducted their transactions; improbable cousins of mountebanks, they would later become known as "bankers."

Most of the great medieval fairs had vanished by the mid-eighteenth century. Big towns did not welcome itinerant performers any more, so the visual entertainers became free wanderers who searched for audiences in village squares. Nevertheless, the best of them managed to find more sedentary employment in the newly developing commercial theaters, such as Sadler's Wells in London or the Théâtre des Funambules in Paris. Between the usual theatrical fare of that period (plays, burlettas, and pantomimes), the jugglers and acrobats displayed their skills, some becoming the true stars of the performance, to the considerable annoyance of more "legitimate" actors. At the same time riding instructors, who had been in the service of privately-funded military regiments, turned trick riders when their aristocrat masters became unable to maintain such extravagances. They took to the road to show their "feats of horsemanship" to increasingly enthusiastic audiences. The fascination with horses may be

Top: The father of the modern circus, Philip Astley. Bottom left: A true international star of the early equestrian circus, the ballerina on horseback Palmyre Annato (c. 1840). Bottom right: The oldest known circus advertisement, for Astley's Riding School (c. 1770).

hard to understand for modern audiences, but remember that for millennia the horse had been man's closest and most indispensable companion, assisting him for transportation, agriculture, hunting, and war. Until the advent of the motor car, everybody had a vested interest in horses and horsemanship.

The birth of the circus

The circus as we know it was created in the late eighteenth century in England by Philip Astley, a former cavalry sergeant-major turned showman. The son of a cabinet maker and veneer cutter, Astley had served during the Seven Years' War in a light dragoon regiment where he displayed an outstanding talent as a horse breaker and trainer. Upon his discharge, he chose to emulate the trick riders who exhibited with tremendous success all over Europe. In England, Price, Johnson, Balp, Coningham, Faulkes, and "Old" Sampson had become fixtures of London's pleasure gardens and inspiration for Astley.

Philip Astley settled in London and opened a riding school near Westminster Bridge on the south bank of the Thames, where he taught in the morning and performed his "feats of horsemanship" in the afternoon. Astley's school featured a circular arena that he called a "circle," or "circus," which would later be known as the "ring." Trick riders had devised the ring some years earlier. Beside allowing the audience to keep sight of the horsemen (not an easy task when they galloped back and forth across open fields), the ring proved ideal for generating the centrifugal force that helped trick riders balance while they stood on the back of their galloping horses. Astley's original ring was about 62 feet in diameter; its size was later reduced to 42 feet, which has since become the international standard for circus rings.

By 1770, Astley's considerable success as a performer outshone his reputation as a teacher. After two seasons in London, however, he needed to bring some novelty to his show. He hired acrobats, rope dancers, and jugglers, whom he found mostly at Sadler's Wells, and interspersed their acts between his equestrian displays. Another addition was a character borrowed from the Elizabethan theater, the clown, who filled

By PARTICULAR DESIRE,
The Whole of thefe amazing various Exhibitions, under the following Titles, viz.
HORSEMANSHIP, or ACTIVITY,
By Mr. and Mrs. ASTLEY, &c. &c. &c.
The BROAD-SWORD as in Real ACTION.
HEAVY BALLANCING, and Horfemanſhip BURLESQU'D.
With a COMIC RACE in Sacks, by Four Capital Performers in that Art.
ALSO,
Comus, Jonas, & Breflaw's Tricks, with Sleeve Buttons, Watches, Purſes, Money, Letters, Cards, &c.
By the Little Learned MILITARY HORSE.
(With a ſhort inſtructive Lecture on each by Mr. ASTLEY.) Alfo
The Magical Tables: Or, the Little Horfe turn'd Conjurer.
In Four GRAND CHANGES.
With Variety of other Exhibitions, to make the General Nights complete.
To begin at a Quarter before Six o'Clock precifely——Admittance One Shilling each, though not the

the pauses between acts with burlesques of juggling, tumbling, tight-rope dancing, and even trick riding. The clown also played short comic scenes and appeared at the end of the show in pantomimes (a mixture of comedy and stage spectacles traditionally involving the clown, along with Harlequin and Columbine, borrowed from the Italian commedia dell'arte) which were then extremely popular on the London stage. Thus, out of the combination of equestrian displays, feats of strength and agility, and comedy, what we now call the classical circus was born.

Astley himself opened Paris's first circus, the Amphithéâtre Anglois, in 1782. That same year he encountered his first competition, from the equestrian Charles Hughes, a former member of his company. Hughes teamed up with Charles Dibdin, a prolific songwriter and author of pantomimes, and together they opened a rival amphi-theater and riding school only a stone's throw from Astley's London theater. Dibdin named it the Royal Circus and Equestrian Philharmonic Academy. The first element of this rather bombastic title was to be adopted as the generic name for the new form of entertainment: the "circus." In 1793, one of Hughes's pupils, John Bill Ricketts, opened the first American circus in Philadelphia. This was indeed a classical circus, on the model conceived by Astley and emulated by Hughes. Five years later Ricketts also established the first Canadian circus in Montreal. The British equestrian Philip Lailson, Ricketts' only competition in the Americas, introduced the circus to Mexico in 1802.

Circus shows were originally performed in buildings built specially for that purpose. Although at first these were usually temporary wooden structures, soon every major European city boasted at least one permanent circus, whose architecture could compete with the most flamboyant theaters. Circus buildings were also erected in the New World's largest cities, including New York, Philadelphia, Montreal, and Mexico City. In Europe, these structures remained the preferred setting for circus performances well into the twentieth century; in the United States, however, the circus adopted a different format.

The American traveling circus

In the early nineteenth century, the United States was a developing nation with few cities important enough to sustain resident circuses. Out on the western frontier, settlers were still on the move, establishing new communities in a constantly-expanding country. To meet their public, showmen had little choice but to travel light and fast. In 1825, an entrepreneur named Joshuah Purdy Brown replaced the usual wooden circus building with a full canvas tent, a system that became commonplace by the mid-1830s. J. Purdy Brown came from the town of Somers, New York, where a cattle dealer named Hachaliah Bailey had purchased a young African elephant that he exhibited over the country with great success. Soon the addition of other exotic animals led to the creation of a bona-fide traveling menagerie, and Bailey's prosperity convinced other farmers from the Somers area to go into the traveling menagerie business — to which some added circus performances. In 1835, a group of 135 enterprising farmers and menagerie owners, mostly from Somers, joined forces to create the Zoological Institute, a trust which controlled thirteen itinerant menageries and three affiliated circuses, thus cornering the country's traveling circus and menagerie business.

These early efforts helped define the American circus: It was a traveling tent show coupled with a menagerie, and run by businessmen. In contrast, European circuses were housed in circus buildings and for the most part remained under the control of

Top: The last classical one-ring circus building in New York, the Hippotheatron, or New
York Circus. It was located on 14th Street at
Union Square, in what was then the heart of
the Theater District. It was destroyed by fire
in 1872. **Below:** Nineteenth century acrobats.
(Drawing by Jules Garnier, c. 1895)

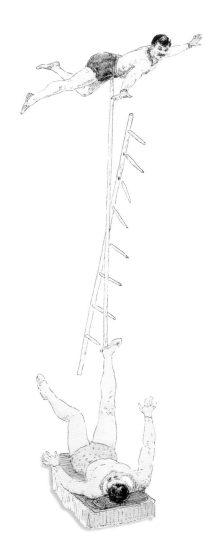

performing families. In 1871, Phineas Taylor Barnum, then retired but still renowned
as an impresario, promoter and museum exhibitor, along with the circus entrepreneur
William Cameron Coup, launched P.T. Barnum's Museum, Menagerie & Circus. The
"museum" part of the entertainment was an exhibition of animal and human oddities, which
soon became an integral element of the American circus: the sideshow. In 1872, Coup
devised a system of daily transportation by rail for their circus; now they could move
more quickly between cities, carry a bigger show, and thus attract bigger audiences.
The show created by Barnum and Coup became the leading enterprise in late nineteenth
century America's most popular form of entertainment by far, the traveling circus.

The one problem faced by Barnum and Coup was that they were turning away
customers: Their tent could only hold a limited number of spectators. Due to the
technical limitations of tent making at the time, the only way to significantly increase
the size of a circus tent, and therefore its capacity, was by adding more poles and
extending its length. But this considerably diminished the visibility for the audience
seated at both ends of the elongated "Big Top." In 1872 Coup added a second ring to
their circus, so that all spectators in the tent could have something to see close to them
— or so was it argued. This innovation was a success, at least as far as profits were
concerned, so in 1881 they added a third ring, and eventually their tents would boast
up to three rings and four stages at the same time. Following Coup's example, nearly
every other large American circus quickly adopted the three ring format, for rea-
sons that had nothing to do with artistry and everything to do with entrepreneurial
greed. Rather than enjoying the skill and artistry of individual artists, the American
circus audience now was presented grand, distant spectacles like human cannonballs
being shot across the tent, colorful pageants, and ever expanding herds of performing
elephants. American entrepreneurs had learned how to make the circus gloriously
profitable, but in doing so they had unconsciously severed themselves from the
artistic tradition that had begun with Philip Astley.

The circus conquers the world

The circus is essentially a visual performing art, unfettered by language barriers. This
gave early circus companies the freedom to embark on extensive international tours.
The most remarkable of these early circus pioneers was the Italian equestrian
Giuseppe Chiarini, who in 1853 sailed for Cuba with his company, established a circus
in Havana, then performed in the United States, crossed the Pacific, and took his circus
to Japan. In 1864 Chiarini settled in Mexico, where he built a circus (which, in 1868,
housed the Mexican Parliament), and from there toured Chile and Argentina, before
returning to Europe and then going to China and Brazil. Next, the company embarked
on a tour of Australia, New Zealand, Tasmania, Singapore, Java, Siam, India, and
South Africa. And so it went, until the 1897 death of the intrepid Italian in Guatemala.

The French equestrian Louis Soullier toured the Balkans, settled for a time in Turkey,
and then continued to China, where he introduced the circus in 1854. When he returned
to Europe, he brought with him Chinese acrobats who introduced traditional Chinese
acts such as perch-pole balancing, diabolo-juggling, plate-spinning, hoop-diving, etc.,
to Western audiences. In 1816, another French equestrian, Jacques Tourniaire, went to
St. Petersburg where he established the first Russian circus. This frenzy of travel caused
the circus to be global long before the word became fashionable, and traditional
circus dynasties to experience some confusion with national identities. TheAustro-

Hungarian equestrian Carl Magnus Hinné established circuses in Frankfurt, Warsaw, Copenhagen, and eventually (in 1868) St. Petersburg and Moscow, where he was later succeeded by his Italian brother-in-law, the flamboyant equestrian and manager Gaetano Ciniselli. Thus the names of Hinné and Ciniselli have become associated with Russia. The French Gautier family is known as a Scandinavian circus dynasty; members of the German Schumann family became a household name in Denmark, although the "Danish" Schumanns actually hold Swedish passports; the first "French" circus dynasty was founded by an Italian, Antonio Franconi; and on and on.

European circus companies ventured into new territories for the financial rewards; this potential was not lost to the big American circus entrepreneurs. Before entering a partnership with P. T. Barnum in 1881, James Anthony Bailey (no relation to the earlier elephant exhibitor) embarked his circus on a trip to Honolulu, the Fiji Islands, Tasmania, the Dutch East Indies, Australia, New Zealand, and South America. After Barnum's death, Bailey took their Barnum & Bailey "Greatest Show On Earth" on an extensive European tour from 1897 to 1902. European circus owners were impressed by Barnum & Bailey's touring techniques, and menagerie owners, whose business was fading at the time, were quick to see the advantage of adding a traveling circus to their zoological exhibitions. Barnum & Bailey's three rings, however, appeared outlandish and confusing to the knowledgeable European circus audiences, who hung on to their one-ring traditions. Thus, while European circus owners were willing to adopt the tented traveling circus and menagerie, the massive three-ring circus remained a uniquely American phenomenon. (When Bailey returned to the United States in 1902, he found his old market under the control of the giant circus conglomerate created by the Ringling brothers. One year after Bailey's 1906 death, the Ringlings acquired Barnum & Bailey, which they combined with their own circus in 1919.)

In Europe, the traveling circus and menagerie reached its peak between the World Wars, especially in Germany where the *kolossal* traveling enterprises of Krone, Sarrasani, and Hagenbeck dominated the European market. Nevertheless, in large cities circus performances were still given in buildings; Paris alone maintained four of them at that time. This created a demanding European audience that had grown accustomed to a high level of comfort and production values at the circus. While in the Unites States the tenting techniques developed by W. C. Coup remained practically unchanged for over a century, European tent makers constantly developed new systems for circus tents and seating, which eventually made some European traveling circuses nearly as comfortable and production-efficient as any permanent building. (In 1981, the Big Apple Circus would be the first to introduce an European-made circus tent to the United States.)

The circus performance

Changes did not occur just to the commercial and physical aspects of the circus. The performance had been constantly evolving since the era of Astley, and by the 1900, the show had fundamentally changed. At its inception, the core of the circus performance was equestrian acts — trick riding, bareback acrobatics, dressage or haute-école, presentation of horses "at liberty," and even comedy on horseback — interspersed with acrobatic, balancing, and juggling acts. Charles Dibdin, Hughes' partner, had made the pantomime an important ingredient of that traditional fare; it traditionally ended the show and came to involve a good amount of tumbling, clowning (not nec-

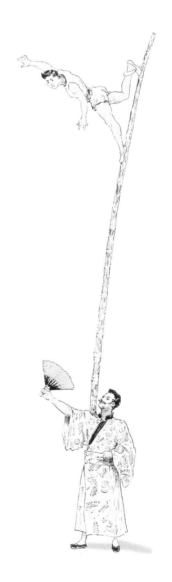

Top: Paris's *Cirque de l'Impératrice* (also known as *Cirque d'Eté*), in 1852. Located on the lower part of the Champs-Elysées, near the "Rond-point," it was a fashionable destination on summer nights. Its winter counterpart, the Cirque d'Hiver, built that same year as the Cirque Napoléon, still stands and is still active in Paris.

essarily mute), and equestrian displays. Pantomimes remained extremely successful during the entire nineteenth century, and survived under various forms well into the twentieth. The last notable circus pantomime was a spectacular adaptation of Lewis Wallace's Ben Hur that the French circus Gruss toured for several years in the 1960s.

Although by the second half of the nineteenth century, equestrians, male and female, were still the true stars of the circus, acrobats were beginning to get real attention. Not surprisingly, it started with acrobats on horseback, especially in the United States, where John H. Glenroy accomplished the first somersault on horseback in 1846. 'Floor' acrobats were also quick to make their mark, the best of them often clowns. Circus clowns had at first been essentially skilled artists — acrobats, jugglers, rope dancers, and dancers. They often performed parodies of equestrian acts, but most of their repertoire consisted of exercises of strength and agility whose apparent eccentricity (in that pre-Olympics era) was considered funny. In the early 1800s, an English clown named Little Wheal became famous for performing regularly one hundred consecutive somersaults in tempo — quite a feat then as now!

Rope dancers had been the fairgrounds' undisputed stars during the seventeenth and eighteenth centuries and were among the first acrobats to appear in the circus ring. There, they developed an adaptation of their art which would eventually become one of the circus' prized attractions: the trapeze. They began by swinging on and hanging from a slack rope, then a bar was added in the middle while the half ropes on each side moved toward a vertical position, giving birth to the trapeze. In 1859, the French gymnast Jules Léotard presented at Paris's Cirque Napoléon (today the Cirque d'Hiver) an act titled *La Course aux Trapèzes*, in which he jumped from one trapeze to another. He thus invented the flying trapeze and became the toast of Europe — as

much for his act as for the revealing costume he originated, the leotard. In this costume, Léotard became one of the great sex symbols of nineteenth century show business.

By the end of the nineteenth century, railways and a new invention called the automobile had begun to replace horses. Although major European circuses were still operated by equestrian families, equestrian displays were losing their supremacy to trainers of exotic animals (especially big cats), acrobats, aerialists, jugglers, and clowns. While a few trained exotic animals had appeared early in circus history (around 1812 the Franconis had presented Kioumi, the first trained elephant, at Paris' Cirque Olympique), in Europe it was the combination of circus and menagerie, along with the expansion of European colonial empires into little known parts of the globe, notably in Africa, which triggered the vogue of wild animal presentations. Another significant factor was a renewed interest in gymnastics and physical activities (which led to the resurrection of the Olympic Games in 1896) at a time when gymnasts could essentially be seen only at the circus.

After World War I, the old equestrian circus was just a memory. Its legendary stars had been replaced by the likes of triple-somersaulter Alfredo Codona on the flying trapeze, Con Colleano dancing on the tight wire, juggling legend Enrico Rastelli, and star-clowns such as the Fratellinis, Grock, and Charlie Rivel. Clowns in Europe remained true to their theatrical ancestry; they were essentially comic actors who could speak, sing, play music, and even comment on current events and tell jokes about politicians. For this reason some of them, like the Russian Anatoly Durov and his brother Vladimir, became wildly popular. In the United States, the clown Dan Rice had been the first nationally recognizable star of the pre-Civil War era. This was before the American circus lost its theatricality to the likes of Barnum, Coup, and Bailey. Afterward, victims of both the size of the tents and the three-ring format, American clowns became speechless characters confined to oversized visual gags.

The most consequential circus innovation of the twentieth century occurred in the Soviet Union, where the circus had always been extremely popular. In 1919, all Russian circuses were nationalized by a decree of Lenin, and the vast majority of performers, natives of Western Europe, quickly fled the country. Faced with the necessity of creating a core of uniquely Russian performers, the Soviet government in 1927 established the State University of Circus and Variety Arts, better known as the Moscow Circus School. Not only did the school inject new blood to the circus, it also developed new training methods modeled after sport-gymnastics, created original presentations with the help of outside directors and choreographers, and even developed innovative techniques and apparatuses that led to the invention of entirely new acts.

When the Moscow Circus (a generic name adopted by all Soviet circus companies touring abroad) started showing in the West in the late 1950s, the training of their performers was obviously superior to the old in-house training of the traditional circus families who provided acts to European and American circuses. Russian performers displayed originality, unparalleled artistry, and amazing technique. The Westerners, in contrast, had been futilely fighting the emerging competition from radio, movies, and television by repeating the same hoary acts whose success, they thought, was time-tested and thus guaranteed. Fear of change had transformed their traditions into routine, and, for the most part, old circus families were losing touch with their audience's ever transforming world. In America, the sheer size of the tents and arenas also encouraged

Below: A nineteenth century poster for the *Cirque d'Eté*, on the Champs-Elysées in Paris (see p. 14). Note the predominance of the equestrian acts on the illustration.

some lazy circus performers to reduce their acts to a few spectacular stunts that could be seen from everywhere in the house. At the same time, they were fighting for the attention of an audience distracted by omnipresent "candy-butchers" hawking cotton-candy and popcorn in the stands. This was the circus as mass entertainment, not as an art form.

This was as far as the New York Public Library's circus history books went. The next chapter was to include Paul Binder, Michael Christensen, and the Big Apple Circus. Although they were only faintly aware of it at the time, they were part of a seismic tremor that was rumbling through circus world in both Europe and the United States.

The circus today

Before the 1970s, there were a few circus producers who were trying to shake up their shows with modernizing lighting, musical accompaniment, staging, and so on. Among them were the Englishman Bertram Mills and his sons, Cyril and Bernard, Jérôme Medrano in Paris, and even John Ringling North in the United States. But fundamental change did not begin until a new generation wholeheartedly accepted the Russian model, with its professional circus schools and innovative circus acts and productions. In 1974, Annie Fratellini (heiress to the famous clowning dynasty) and Alexis Gruss, Jr. (heir to the last French equestrian dynasty) created in Paris the first two Russian-inspired circus schools in the Western world. Their respective performing departments were circuses where creation was paramount, albeit in both cases within a classical frame. Alexis Gruss defined his style (and subtitled his circus) as *Le Cirque à l'Ancienne* — The Old Time Circus.

This development came not coincidentally at a time when European intellectuals, mostly French, were fretting over the decline of the circus as a performing art. In 1975, Prince Rainier of Monaco, a long-time circus enthusiast, created the International Circus Festival of Monte-Carlo, whose Gold and Silver Clown awards have become to the circus world what the Oscar is to the movie industry. It was followed in 1977 by Paris' Festival Mondial du Cirque de Demain (World Festival of the Circus of Tomorrow) created to showcase and promote the new generation of circus performers, most of them trained in circus schools. In this new atmosphere, the Gruss/Fratellini example quickly stimulated other experiments. In 1977, Bernhard Paul and André Heller created the Circus Roncalli in Germany, restoring on a more intimate scale the lost flamboyance of the German circus of yore. In Montreal, Guy Caron founded the Ecole Nationale de Cirque (National Circus School) in 1980, which was followed in 1984 by Guy Laliberté's very innovative Cirque du Soleil, whose first Artistic Director was Caron. And, of course, in 1977 Paul Binder and Michael Christensen, who had experienced first-hand the Fratellini/Gruss experiments when they performed their juggling act at Annie Fratellini's Nouveau Cirque de Paris, created the Big Apple Circus. Like Fratellini and Gruss in Europe, Paul and Michael wanted to re-introduce in the United States the one-ring, theatrical circus: in fact, the original American circus.

The circus mavericks of the 1970s and 1980s were outsiders whose enterprises, each in its own way, were highly creative shows that gave a much needed boost to the circus arts. They had a major influence in changing the artistic and commercial attitude of many more traditional circuses, and, more importantly, in the development of a "new circus" movement that redefined the circus as a performing art.

D.J.

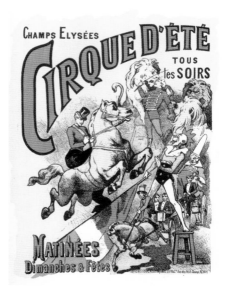

The Little Show that Could: the beginnings

Photo: Peter Angelo Simon

Great adventures often begin as the result of chance encounters. The genesis of the Big Apple Circus is no exception. What could have caused a Brooklyn-born MBA and a young actor from Walla Walla, Washington, to team up and create one of the world's most celebrated circuses? Chance is the only possible answer.

Paul Binder was born and raised in a Jewish family in the Flatbush section of Brooklyn. His mother ran the household while his father was the sales manager of a top New York State winery. Paul's father had an artistic side, too; he loved playing the violin and for a while he conducted his own dance band. Like many city kids, Paul was occasionally taken to the circus at Madison Square Garden. "I do have one very powerful memory,"Paul says, "a spotlighted Unus, alone in the center ring, doing his one-finger-stand on a lighted globe. It was very dramatic!" However, the idea that within the circus ring would lie his career never entered his mind. Paul attended Dartmouth, where he joined the Dartmouth Players and the Hopkins Center Repertory Theatre, and then earned his MBA at Columbia University. After a brief stint at Boston University's School of Fine and Applied Arts, he went to work as stage manager for Julia Child and later as talent coordinator for Merv Griffin's television show. Nevertheless, it was the end of the 1960s, and Paul was restless with the times.

Meanwhile in Walla Walla, Washington, where he was born, Michael Christensen was struggling with a difficult childhood — an unhappy, dysfunctional home life, mercifully compensated for by generally pleasant experiences outside his home and at school. Somehow Michael needed to act out some of the feelings stirred by this uneasy life, so quite naturally he enrolled in the Professional Actor Training program at the University of Washington. Michael became an actor. As for the circus: "When the circus came to town in the summer, I helped setting up the tents with my brother, in exchange for free passes. I also remember laughing uncontrollably at a clown gag — but I don't remember who the clown was nor what was the gag!"

Top: Paul wanders into the ring of the newly-born Big Apple Circus. **Below:** The San Francisco Mime Troupe in performance. Michael is the third clown from the left (with a bald wig). **Previous page:** Michael as Zakahr.

Photo: Gerhard E. Gscheidle

Top: In the early days of the Big Apple Circus, Michael and Paul appeared with their juggling act in several episodes of Sesame Street.

Both Michael and Paul ended up in San Francisco, where they met at the San Francisco Mime Troupe. During the late 1960s and early 1970s, San Francisco was the epicenter of a whole rebellious era of student revolt and social change. The San Francisco Mime Troupe was taking an active part in that change, through a political street theater movement aimed at stimulating people through outrageous, right-in-your-face physicality. Michael, the aspiring, angry actor, found a natural niche in the Mime Troupe. Paul was also in a rebellious mood then and needed to act out his frustrations. He received a warm welcome in the troupe, although his MBA was perhaps more attractive to them than his college theatrical past.

One of the techniques used by the Mime Troupe to convey their messages was juggling. Michael and Paul learned juggling, and notably "passing" (two or more jugglers passing objects back and forth) with co-member Larry Pisoni, with whom Michael developed a juggling comedy routine. Pisoni would go on to become the founder of San Francisco's celebrated Pickle Family Circus, and a great American clown. One day, Larry and Michael decided to go and see the world. They would do their "grand tour," as the wealthy European youth of centuries past had done, and survive by juggling on street corners, as the wealthy European youth had certainly never done. Michael flew to London first, but soon after Larry let him know that he could not go. It was a letdown, but Michael did not want to return home empty-handed. Luckily, Paul heard of the situation and called Michael to offer himself as a replacement. He and Michael had been occasional juggling partners, and he was familiar with Larry and Michael's routine. Michael was relieved, and Paul flew to London. Thus began the now-legendary juggling journey of Paul Binder and Michael Christensen through the big cities and one-horse towns of Europe.

A juggling journey

It was a journey of many magical encounters and discoveries, some of which would be prophetic. In Paris, they met and befriended a fellow street performer (there were only a few of them at the time) named Philippe Petit. Later, in 1974, Philippe managed to string a cable between the tops of the not-yet-completed twin towers of the World Trade Center, walk cross the world's highest tightrope, and become instantly famous.

On the road, Paul and Michael developed a very good passing act, in which talking was as important as juggling. They adapted their spoken comedy to the language of the countries they visited, and the act was generally funnier in its foreign versions — half the humor was these two young Americans stumbling through the native tongue of their audience. They passed traditional clubs and occasionally a rubber chicken named "Leonard." They became very successful, and their work generated good money, at least in places where there was money. Sometimes, however, it also generated the local authorities' suspicion, as wandering entertainers have always been threatening to the established order.

In Greece, then under a dictatorship, they were taken to a police station where they were confronted with an officer they took for the spitting image — fast, mustachioed, and sweating — of Sergeant Garcia from the old *Zorro* television series. When the officer asked the arresting cop what had brought these young Americans to his office, the cop explained with much visual aid (in the form of mime-like gesticulations) that they had been juggling in the streets, thus disturbing the public order. Taking his cue from the visual part of the explanation, Paul thought it would help to demonstrate and started juggling balls, one of which accidentally bounced on the head of "Sergeant Garcia." They owed their freedom to a staff member of the U.S. Consulate who advised them that Greece was not a great country for street jugglers, and that they had best head for the border.

Finally, Paul and Michael reached Istanbul and the Bosporus. On the other side of the strait lay Asia, the Orient, the unknown. "I burst into tears," Paul says, "I was sure that on the other side of that water was madness. We were crazy enough already." They decided it was time to reverse their path, so they juggled their way back to Paris.

Chance encounters: Michael and Paul were performing their act on the Boulevard Saint-Germain when a man who worked as a theater usher approached them. Would they be interested in auditioning for Roland Petit? The famous choreographer was then artistic director of the Casino de Paris, and the legendary revue theater starred his wife, Zizi Jeanmaire. Why not? In front of Roland Petit, the duo performed their act honed on the streets of Europe: comic juggling involving a rubber chicken named Leonard, with all dialogue spoken in American-accented French. It was pure novelty! Paul and Michael appeared at the Casino de Paris, and from there they were booked onto French television. France had only three television channels then, so an appearance on any of them meant big exposure. And by chance, Annie Fratellini and Pierre Etaix happened to be watching the show.

Annie Fratellini was the granddaughter of Paul Fratellini, of the legendary clown trio of François, Paul, and Albert Fratellini, and the daughter of Victor Fratellini, himself a clown (like all subsequent Fratellinis). From World War I through the 1940s, François, Paul, and Albert Fratellini were as famous in Europe as, say, the Marx Brothers were in America, and more so. In France, they were truly mythic characters; for them, Jean Cocteau wrote a farce, *Le Boeuf sur le Toit*, and Alexander Calder fabricated a surrealistic articulated wire "dog" for Albert. Annie Fratellini had been a cabaret and music-hall entertainer and a movie actress. Her husband, Pierre Etaix, had been Jacques Tati's assistant (and the designer of his iconic poster for *Mon Oncle*) before writing and directing his own comedies. Like Tati, Etaix was fascinated by the circus and by clowns, whom he often used to act in his movies. He convinced Annie, who had starred in his aptly titled film, *Le Grand Amour*, to return to her clowning roots, and together they created what was to become a legendary clown duet. They were also in the process of developing a professional circus school and a circus. They called Michael and Paul: Would they like to participate in a show they were putting together? Would they like to be part of the first tour of their Nouveau Cirque de Paris? "Yes, why not?" was the answer to both questions.

This chance encounter turned into an epiphany. "Everything led to and came from that experience," says Paul. Adds Michael: "What I believe led Paul to vocalizing the idea for the Big Apple Circus was the joy that we felt in doing this work. There was a tremendous amount of joy that we felt with each other as we worked in the streets and living this wonderful adventure. But that paled to the joy and the feeling of a home that we had found when we peeked through those curtains into the wonderful world of the one-ring circus. And not just any one-ring circus: It was the circus that Pierre Etaix and Annie Fratellini were spinning out of their hearts and the spirit of the clowns they were that really spoke to who we are, who we have always been, and I hope who we'll always be.

Top: The wonderful Annie Fratellini, as her clown persona, sitting on the ring curb of the Nouveau Cirque de Paris (1975).

Photos: Marc Etaix

I remember so clearly looking at Paul and Paul looking at me, and saying, 'Do you believe it? We are in the circus!' And that is still very much alive. It finds its way into things you can't ever imagine." Paul continues: "We learned what a well-planned and well-executed circus could bring to both the people in it and the audience that it serves. And that is a part of the vision of the Big Apple Circus: Circus is something very special that needs to be nurtured and given as a gift to the audience — with a sense of joy and, dare I say, love. It always has to be present for a circus to truly touch people's lives."

Seeds of a circus

The first part of the journey had come to an end. Paul was homesick. At the end of the Nouveau Cirque de Paris' summer season, he returned to New York City. Since their act was already hired for the Christmas season, Michael stayed in France and went to help the vendanges, the harvest of wine grapes, in the southwest of France. "Although I drank lots of it," muses Michael, "I can't recall the name of the wine."

One morning, Paul woke up in his Manhattan loft with a brainstorm that he immediately shared with his cat: Why not create in New York a classical, one-ring circus, with the same intimacy, warmth, dedication, and artistry that he and Michael had experienced in France? It would come with a school to feed the production, as Fratellini had done, and it would play the parks. To his cat, Paul announced: "The New York School for Circus Arts presents The Big Apple Circus!" Paul liked the sound of it, and the cat smiled, or so Paul says. And, as he recalls, "I had the feeling from the beginning that we should bring to it components of service to the community that worked with the same principle. The joy and satisfaction that we knew in the ring could be brought into peoples' lives in other ways."

On his birthday in October of 1976, Paul gathered some friends and unveiled his idea. They reacted to it more joyfully and vocally than his cat, and Paul realized that something there really touched a chord. As Peter Angelo Simon, the Big Apple Circus's first chronicler and photographer, quoted Paul saying later: "There's a reason why everyone was drawn or came to the Big Apple Circus — to find something of themselves that they couldn't find without it."* For some time, there had been a movement toward the rebirth of classical circus in America, one that was different from both the gigantic corporate affair that was Ringling Bros. and Barnum & Bailey and the pathetic remnants of the defunct golden era of the three-ring Big Top. In New York, Hovey Burgess, who had taught juggling to Larry Pisoni (who in turn taught Michael and Paul), had been instrumental in triggering this movement. In San Francisco, Larry Pisoni, Peggy Snider, Cecil McKinnon, Judy Finelli, and other alumni of Burgess's studio were already experimenting with the Pickle Family Circus. Even though the idea was obviously a great one, however, the journey was not going to be easy.

Friends came to help, some attracted by the prospect of being physically part of a circus, others by this unconventional concept of creating a resident circus in New York City. When Paul returned to Paris for the Christmas season, he had already set the wheels in motion. He met Michael in a café and, sipping a *grand crème*, told him that they were in the process of raising a quarter of a million dollars to create their own circus. "Do you want to help me?" Michael ordered another *grand crème*, tried to make sense of what he had just heard, and said, "Sure! And I will do a trained mole act." Paul never asked what he had on his mind; it just remained a big question mark. They went on to juggle their last season at the Nouveau Cirque de Paris, and then Michael and Paul returned to Manhattan.

*: Peter Angelo Simon, *Big Apple Circus*, New York: Penguin Books, 1978

Previous page, top: Annie Fratellini, with Pierre Etaix as the white-face clown, in the ring of the Nouveau Cirque de Paris. Bottom: Paul and Michael rush into the ring for the finale at the Nouveau Cirque de Paris. Annie Fratellini is on the right.

Photo: Fred de Van

As an investor, I was attracted to the idea of a circus bringing high-quality live family entertainment to New York City. The self-contained tent and seating seemed to offer the possibility of an efficient way for doing what other media could not do. There are very few intimate live family experiences that can do what the Big Apple Circus does in a tent seating 2000.

I was attracted to the Big Apple Circus by Paul and Michael, at a time when the circus was only an idea. I was asked to help fund the first tent, seating 600 and costing about $60,000. They were young and full of enthusiasm, their juggling act was really terrific, and the street audiences who saw it were captivated.

They showed me beautiful pictures of European single-ring circuses. It was a venture capital deal — I was buying into their know-how, their dreams, and their passion, and seemingly their capacity. It was the best investment I ever made.

Practice enhancing coexistence in your daily life. Make advancing coexistence in your community your priority. Become a coexistence leader.

Alan B. Slifka

Money realities

Richard Levy was a closet juggler and, in public, an economist and teacher with a keen interest in politics and sociology. When Paul told him of his dream, Richard was quick to see what such a circus could bring to the life of the city, which then teetered on the edge of bankruptcy. He became the project's champion and its chief fund-raiser. In his conversations with Paul, however, he played the devil's advocate, trying to bring Paul's dreams back to the real world. He nevertheless put up his own house as a security for a loan — for a circus that existed only on paper.

While Paul had been in Paris, Richard had gotten various balls in motion. He found someone a little more cool-headed than the dreamers who surrounded them to write what he called a "killer proposal." Her name was Carol Brightman. She would collaborate with Paul, Michael, Richard, and another friend, Julie Winter, on what was to become the key document. This proposal was necessary to seek financial help from businesses, city and state agencies, and in general people who, unlike them, were used to dealing with projects on a more solid basis than sheer impulse.

Another series of chance encounters: Maggie Heimann was "a dynamo . . . an incredibly well organized woman."* Maggie Heimann also knew a lot of people and told Richard and Paul: "Use my name." She opened doors to William Woodward, a self-effacing civic leader who studied the killer proposal, listened to Paul's pitch, sat through the slide-show illustrating Annie Fratellini's circus and school, and instantly became a true believer. She also brought Virginia and Alan Slifka, a soft-spoken, successful investment banker with a vague resemblance to Jimmy Stewart, to a rehearsal at the Spring Street studio (of which more later). Slifka then went through the killer proposal, the pitch, and the slide show. His response was: "My wife and I think it's a wonderful idea. We'd like to help." Maggie Heimann, William Woodward, and Alan Slifka were soon lured onto the first board of directors of the newly formed not-for-profit organization, the New York School for Circus Arts, Inc. And Alan and Virginia Slifka would help indeed: Alan would remain its Chairman of the Board and guiding light for the next 15 years, and he and Virginia would help the organization weather many a financial crisis. Alan remains active today as Chairman Emeritus.

At first, sponsors were not easy to find. After all, the project existed mainly on paper and proposed the unfamiliar concept of a linked circus and circus school. The first corporation to back the idea was Con Edison, which pledged $25,000 to open the first season's matinee shows to children from poor neighborhoods who could not afford tickets. This corresponded to Paul and Michael's sense of community service (and it guaranteed that at least someone would see the shows!). It was also the birth of what was to become the Big Apple Circus' Ticket Fund and later, Circus For All!® Michael and Paul also raised funds with performances in both the parks and at luxurious homes out in the Hamptons. In Washington Square Park, they renewed their friendship with Philippe Petit, who often performed there and was now world-famous and a New York icon after his stunt at the World Trade Center. Although quite an individualist, Philippe was ready to help.

Russian teachers

Meanwhile the school itself took shape. An artist with a fondness for the circus, Karen Gersch had learned to juggle with Hovey Burgess, practiced acrobatics, and nursed clowning ambitions. She fell in love with the project and put her 17th Street loft, which

*Peter Angelo Simon, Ibid.

was already a magnet for jugglers and acrobats in need of practice space, at the disposal of the performers and would-be performers who were enrolling in the project. Karen also brought in a couple of Russian immigrants she had met recently and who she believed could help. Another chance encounter.

Top: Still struggling to make a living, Michael and Paul perform their juggling act in Manhattan's Washington Square. (On the left, Leonard is sitting on Michael's head.) **Left:** Nina Krasavina and Gregory Fedin in one of their favorite positions. **Below:** Nina Krasavina peeking through the curtain.

In 1974, Gregory Fedin and Nina Krasavina had left the USSR and arrived pennyless in New York City. They were professional circus performers. In an attempt to find a job, they managed to have their picture printed in a newspaper, showing Nina doing a one-arm stand on Gregory's head. Karen saw the picture, called the newspaper, and established contact with the couple. They had been in the Soviet circus for 20 years, Nina as a clown, Gregory as an acrobat. In the Soviet Union, the circus was taken seriously indeed as a performing art, and its performers were the best trained in the world and immensely creative. In fact, the visits to the United States of the Moscow Circus had led to the renewal of interest in the circus arts. Paul had been impressed by the Moscow Circus' artistry when it performed at Madison Square Garden's Felt Forum. Like all Soviet circus performers, Nina and Gregory were true artists, worthy models to emulate.

Born in Leningrad, Nina had been a child dancer and studied acrobatics and then clowning. She was rather self-effacing but had a keen eye, could always make good sense of everything, and was blessed with boundless energy. More the extrovert, Gregory did the talking. He was a graduate of the Moscow State Circus School and had worked in the legendary balancing act of Yevgeny Milaev, a major star of the Soviet circus (and also Leonid Brezhnev's son-in-law). Nina and Gregory thought, dreamed, and breathed circus. Nina was quick to see the problems with the traditional American circus: "The three-ring circus allows only for fireworks. The beautiful, subtle art of the individual is lost. America has lost many [circus specialties] because its circus has no real ring!"* When Paul described their project, Gregory expressed his opinion in typically Russian direct fashion: "You want to start a circus? You must work twenty-eight hours a day! You must steal four hours from your death!"*

Nina and Gregory became the New York School for Circus Arts' first

Top left: A rehearsal in the Spring Street "studio." Warren Bacon is the left "bottom man" of the center pyramid; Michael Moschen is the "bottom man" on the right.
Top right: Paul holds a meeting under the brand-new, ill-fitting Big Top. Michael is on the left, leaning pensively on a pole.

Photos: Peter Angelo Simon

teachers. At first, they came only four days a week to Karen's loft. Then Nina, always the realist, and uncompromising where circus arts were involved, asked: "Where is school?" Good question. She stressed that true circus training demands seven days a week and twelve hours a day. A slightly larger space was found on Spring Street, in a storefront owned by theater wunderkind Robert Wilson. Now the school had a home of its own.

Students — potential performers — came. Among them were a group of kids, age 14 to 16, from Charles Evans Hughes High School; they practiced tumbling at a YMCA and were brought in by their teacher. Darryl Hamilton, Steve Johnson, Wayne Jones, Abel Shark, Nat Suares, and Chris Thomas were to become the Back Street Flyers, a staple of the Big Apple Circus' early productions. Five years later they would win a Silver Medal at the Festival Mondial du Cirque de Demain in Paris, bringing the circus world's attention to "the little circus that could" over there in New York. Paul also sought potential performers in the circus world. In Paris, he and Michael had met Los Indianos, an energetic group of Argentinian sabateo dancers. They had become friends, and, when asked, Los Indianos agreed to come. Michael Moschen, a young, very creative, and elegant juggler, joined the company. So did Paul Lubera, a flamboyant trapeze artist, and Suzanne Perry, an out-of-work aerialist who kept a day-job as secretary. Then, of course, Michael and Paul would do their juggling act, and the Back Street Flyers were preparing a tumbling act. Nina and Gregory would take care of the clowning and also perform a spectacular perch-pole balancing act that they had created back in Russia. The Spring Street studio was not high enough for them to practice, so Richard Levy arranged for them to rehearse on the stage of the famous Studio 54 disco (a former theater) during the daytime while the club was being cleaned.

As promised in Paris, Michael was preparing his parody of a trained animal act as Zakahr, the fearless trainer of Gittha, the underground soldier mole... Chance encounters: Jessie Hentoff, a senior student of the school, told Paul about Warren Bacon, an aerialist who knew circus tents and rigging. When Paul contacted him, he was performing in a Taiwan thrill show. Although Warren had gone through a disappointing experience with the Ringling show, this seemed to be the kind of circus he had dreamed of, and he flew back to New York.

A tent had been ordered. The design followed the Nouveau Cirque de Paris' circular, European-style Big Top, but more from guess recollections than thorough technical study. It was being made in Queens, and from the start inexperience and bad communications ran the project into trouble. Making a circus tent is not an easy matter, and more so if one does not hire a professional and experienced tent maker. But budget considerations and unflappable optimism made everybody believe the home-made tent could — must — work.

Richard Levy also brought in Mimi Gross Grooms, an artist and the wife of Red Grooms; she conceived and painted the front banners for the circus and designed the ring entrance. And, most importantly, a circus ring was being built — the altar and epicenter of that traveling town center-cum-cathedral that is a true circus. For the historical record, the first ring of the Big Apple Circus was designed and built by Jim Wintner and John Page.

Raising the tent

Everything was now in motion for a July 4, 1977 opening (it had originally been planned for June). But where? The first choice had been Battery Park at Manhattan's southern tip, but that was without reckoning on New York City's gargantuan bureaucracy. One month before the expected opening, the site had moved from the green lawns of Battery Park to a barren, sand- and gravel-covered landfill on the shores of the Hudson River. It had hopefully been named Battery Park City, but as yet the lot only held piles of illegally dumped garbage. And there was no assurance that the endless list of authorizations and permits would be obtained in time, if ever. Michael Davidson, the circus's brave production manager, even had to buy insurance to cover the damage the tent could cause to the gravel and garbage. And then, what tent? Its maker had gone incommunicado, and nobody knew when it would be delivered.

A week or two prior to the scheduled opening, an exhilarated Davidson announced that he had at last secured all the necessary permits. The rental truck was filled with the ring (but no tent), the permits, show tickets, box-office material, and equipment,

Top left: The landfill behind the chain-link fence will one day be known as Battery Park City. At this moment, however, Paul and Michael see it as a possible paradisaical setting for the Big Apple Circus... Top right: The New York School for Circus Arts studio on Spring Street.

Photos: Peter Angelo Simon

Photos: Peter Angelo Simon

and everyone rushed to the site. When the warden tried to open the chain-fence gates, however, the padlock was stuck. After a series of increasingly violent attempts at unlocking it, it finally succumbed to a pair of cable cutters. At last! As Peter Angelo Simon beautifully put it: "The spirit of the Big Apple Circus entered upon the land."* Then everybody returned to the truck. It had been stolen!

As a dark cloud settled over everyone involved in the Big Apple Circus dream, they soon discovered that a special angel always looks after true circus folks. The police miraculously found the truck and all its contents on East 47th Street, where it had been abandoned by the drunk who had taken it joyriding. Then Michael, Paul, Nina, and Gregory went to Queens to take delivery of the Big Top. They were given the poles, the cables, and the stakes. As for the tent itself, they were told it had been sent to Boston for some "final touches." They all looked at each other. Would there ever be a Big Apple Circus? Was the entire enterprise doomed from the start?

Yet hope can move mountains. Rehearsals continued in earnest at the Spring Street studio. In Manhattan, Paul had watched kids playing in a city playground; their joyous energy, he thought, reflected the true spirit of New York! He asked Nina to create a charivari, the joyful acrobatic ensemble that traditionally opened circus performances in the old days, in that same playground spirit. The students and all the company members were involved.

Michael Moschen endlessly polished his ball and torch routines. At Studio 54, Gregory again and again climbed a pole, with a tall perch pole balancing on his head, atop of which Nina herself was hand-balancing. With Warren Bacon coaching them, the Back Street Flyers were perfecting their new tumbling and mini-tramp act. Los Indianos arrived in New York, true to their word, ready to start the season. But there was still no Big Top. July 4th came. It was a day of fireworks over Manhattan — but no Circus Day! Finally, at 5:30 a.m. on July 9, the tent was delivered to Battery Park City. Impending despair suddenly gave way to relief, excitement, and elation. The poles had been up for a while; even the ring was in position; and the bleachers were piled up nearby. Warren Bacon and his team, and practically everyone available, began the arduous process of setting up a Big Top for the first time.

A first setup is always a period of trial and error, but this one was particularly frustrating. Nothing seemed to fit. It finally become apparent that something was inherently wrong with the tent. After many unsuccessful attempts, changes of technique, new measurements, brain storms, wasted energy, and much too much sweat in the July heat, Warren came to the only obvious conclusion: The measurements had been wrong, and the tent was too small.

Philippe Petit, who was an expert rigger, came to the rescue. He conceived a way to rig the defective tent in spite of its miscalculated size. Two weeks after its delivery, the Big Apple Circus's green Big Top was finally raised! In the meantime, on July 13, New York was victim of its worst power failure in history, leading to a complete blackout. Luckily, Con Edison did not back out of its grant, but that was about the only thing that had gone right.

Finally, on July 18, 1977, with the administrative help of Jill Kirschenbaum, and of her close friend Rob Libbon who figured out how to put up the bleachers, the Big Apple Circus gave its very first performance. Richard Levy and Paul Binder were the show's producers, and Paul also directed. Nina Krasavina was the Artistic Director; Michael

Top: The Back Street Flyers receive a Silver Medal at the 1982 Festival Mondial du Cirque de Demain in Paris, putting the Big Apple Circus on the international circus map. Sacha Pavlata and Paul Binder proudly stand on the right. (Left, Dominique Jando, who just presented the medal, doesn't yet know that one year later he will join the Big Apple Circus staff.) Bottom: The opening "charivari" of the first Big Apple Circus show.

Top: The Big Apple Circus' very first Big Top stands proudly before the twin towers of the World Trade Center. The clown between the legs of the giant cutout clown is Nina Krasavina. Opposite page: Although the fate of the tent is still unknown, the brand-new ring, at least, is delivered to the circus' Battery Park City lot.

Christensen, the Associate Director; and Gregory Fedin, the Artistic Consultant. Louisa Chase had designed the costumes; Mimi Gross Grooms, the set; and Candice Brightman and Jan Kroeze, the lighting. Peter Gordon led the band, and Phil Crowder was the Ringmaster. In the small printed program with a yellow cover, the Big Apple Circus' creators stated their credo:

Our show is the product of dedicated performers who have witnessed the vitality of the circus throughout the world, but bemoan the state of our craft in this country. We have chosen New York City because it is our home and because we know it to be a great resource center which, like the circus, is reborn each generation. By their very nature, the skills of the circus performer are representations of the vitality of human aspirations under challenge: the trapeze artist "flies" against nature; the clown falls, rises, falls, rises — undaunted; the acrobats learn to give and take to maintain balance; "juggling," it has been said, "is the will to survive," to keep objects moving under all circumstances. We dedicate this show to the people of New York City.

And the show went on! Amazingly, 45,000 people attended the Big Apple Circus during its first, 10-week season. With very little advance publicity (for a circus), they found the green tent on its hot and windy stretch of landfill, paid their admission, and, most importantly, loved the show. They got it. They understood why this was not a three-ring extravaganza, and why, in many ways, this might be a better version of a circus. The Daily News said: *The greatest show on earth it ain't. No chorus cuties dancing at the end of their ropes, nary a jeweled tiger or painted elephant to be seen. Just lots of funny clowns, acrobats, tumblers and trapeze artists. And something else—an intimacy with the audience that is hard to beat.* The Village Voice continued: *Part of the fun came from the closeness and the reduced scale. Paul Lubera's trapeze act wasn't all that high above us (although a fall from it could kill him adequately, I'm sure), but he touched the top of the tent when he swung, and a frail spotlight played tricks with his shadows, and your heart did a jump when he suddenly slipped down to hang from one knee . . . The antics of clown-acrobats (apprentices from the school) and the mini-tramp vaultings of six high school kids who call themselves the Back Street Flyers were not only clear and bright and well-timed but close enough for you to feel the texture of the energy.*

Top: Mia Wolff and Dona Farina performed their aerial act in the second season of the Big Apple Circus. **Above:** Michael and Paul in their juggling act. **Bottom left:** A ticket for a performance of the first season. **Bottom right:** The Big Apple Circus Company in a television appearance: (l. to r.) Host, Michael Moschen, Jim and Tisha Tinsman, Michael as Mr. Stubs, Barry Lubin, Mia Wolff, Paul, Dona Farina, and David Dimitri. **Opposite page:** The inimitable Michael Moschen.

The reviewers acknowledged some roughness around the edges but nevertheless raved over Nina and Gregory's clowning, Paul and Michael's flying clubs, the energetic sabateo dancing of Los Indianos, the suave juggling of Michael Moschen, and on and on. And they saw the world's first and only trained mole act: *"We were even treated to a very funny animal act not on the program . . . in which a fierce 'tribesman' of some sort (Christensen) put a dangerous 'soldier mole' (a lump scurrying under the carpet) through its paces."* [Village Voice]

And most importantly, the reviewers saw what the Big Apple Circus had done for the city. The New York Post declared: *"For 90 minutes, New York turns into a village on fair day, binding adults and children alike in a community of sheer pleasure."* The Voice's reviewer said: *"The Big Apple Circus makes me imagine what it must have been like when a small traveling circus hit a small town—everyone in the audience knowing each other and the strange artists inspiring dinner-table talk and trips to the library and playground stunts for months afterward."* On both the artistic level and the more spiritual level of simply bringing people together, the Big Apple Circus was a success. Now if they could only make it financially.

The following summer, the Circus pitched its tent on an empty lot on Eighth Avenue — the site of the old Madison Square Garden! The organization was becoming a little more professional. Names appeared on the board of directors roster that would remain there for years, including Richard Levy, Ruth Shuman, and the Very Reverend James Parks Morton (Dean of the Cathedral Church of St. John The Divine). And Con Edison was still supporting the Ticket Fund. Nina and Gregory were again co-directing and participating in the show, although they were now teaching in their own studio. The New York Times, which up until then had only reviewed the "Big One," finally noticed the show, with an over-the-top rave:

In one sunny tent, the Big Apple Circus of New York demonstrates the theater's own fortunate economy of scale. Pitched from a 38-foot, ridge-pole on the Eighth Avenue parking lot that once held Madison Square Garden and the three-ring Ringling Bros. Circus, the Big Apple accomplishes something quite different. Sometimes awkwardly, sometimes a trifle self-consciously, but altogether winningly, it is the circus of picture-books and tribal memory. A sea of children and a flooded archipelago of adults sit in the single ring under a breathing green canvas, as if they were the iris on an eye whose vision is focused individually and on one thing at a time.

Yet it was not easy for the little circus that could. The season was too short and did not generate enough money to keep the organization afloat for the rest of the year. In 1979, the New York School for Circus Arts introduced an arts-in-education program to provide inner-city kids with in-school circus arts training. But the Big Apple Circus did not perform. Hence came a time of drastic decisions: Should it fold the tent once and for all? Or should it pull out all the stops, find more money, and gather the right people to help fully develop both the circus and the school. The Big Apple's directors chose the latter — a heroic choice involving high risks. It was go or bust.

An Executive Director was hired. Judith Friedlaender was a lawyer who worked in the office of Mayor Koch, and whom Paul had met and converted while trying to secure a site for the Circus. Like Maggie Heimann, Judith knew a lot of people. She was also smart, hard-working, with unbounded energy and dedication.

In the summer of 1980, the Big Apple Circus resurfaced at Gateway National Recreational Area, in Brooklyn. Meanwhile, a new Big Top had been ordered, this time from a professional tentmaker in Italy. This was a necessity since Judith had just hit the jackpot: The Big Apple Circus had obtained from the Lincoln Center for the Performing Arts, the country's undisputed cultural center, the authorization to put up its tent for the Christmas season at Damrosch Park!

The Big Apple Circus gave its first performance at Lincoln Center on December 4, 1981. This was the big time, so big-time performers were hired. The featured attractions were Philippe Petit, with his beautiful high-wire act, and the Flying Gaonas, the greatest flying act of the time, led by the charismatic triple-somersaulter Tito Gaona. The celebrated Danish equestrienne Katja Schumann, heiress to the legendary Schumann circus dynasty, and whom Paul had seen in France, came from Europe and graced the ring with an elegant "high-school" act on her magnificent Arabian stallion, Sky Warrior. There were also the Bertinis, a renowned troupe of Czechoslovakian acrobats on unicycles; Carol Buckley and her baby elephant, Tarra; Sacha Pavlata (also the new tent master and the new School's head-teacher) came from Paris to perform on the cloud swing. Other newcomers joined the resident company, including the hand-balancer Jim Tinsman and his wife, the beautiful Tisha, on the Spanish Web. And Michael Moschen, the Back Street Flyers, and, of course Michael and Paul, completed the line-up.

The show was a triumph, universally praised by New York's theater critics. The only casualty was Zakkahr and his invisible trained mole, Gittha. One, perhaps ironic, reviewer questioned the rationale for the presence in the show of a trained animal the audience could not even see. The critic's humor was lost on Zakkhar, however. Hurt, Michael never presented Gittha again.

25 years On

The Big Apple Circus has built its permanent place in the cultural landscape of New York City. In 1983, it received an OBIE award for Outstanding Achievement in the Theater. It began to leave Manhattan for tours of the boroughs, and then came a season in Boston, which has become its second home. From there it has traveled the world, or at least the eastern half of the United States, with regular performances in Washington, D.C., Atlanta, Chicago, Charlestown, Rhode Island, and Hanover, New Hampshire, among other cities.

New, generous, dedicated, and indefatigable supporters have joined the Big Apple Circus Board of Directors. And the organization has been led by a glittering succession of executive directors, each of whom helped develop a particular area: Elizabeth I. McCann, one of Broadway's finest theatrical producers; the late James C. McIntyre, who came from Carnegie Hall; and Gary Dunning, the present executive director, who hailed from the American Ballet Theater.

Twenty-five years have passed since the Big Apple Circus' small, ill-designed, and ragged green tent opened to the public for the first time at Battery Park City, in the shadow of the World Trade Center. Many chance encounters have happened since. There have been triumphs. There have been tragedies. And the show still goes on.

D.J.

Top: The first poster. Opposite page: The Big Apple Circus first European-made tent in Baltimore, Maryland. The two small silhouettes on the top of the tent, at the left end of the cupola, are Philippe Petit and Judith Friedlaender.

Photo: Theo O. Krath

Top: (form l. to r.) Dominique Jando, Jan Kroeze, Paul (seated), Mummenschanz's Bernie Schurch, and Michael during a rehearsal of *Grandma Meets Mummenschanz*. **Middle, top:** Paul gives rehearsal notes to the cast, with Dominique Jando at his side. **Middle, bottom:** Lighting designer Jan Kroeze at work. **Bottom:** Musical director Rik Albani, and composer Linda Hudes during their long collaboration with the Big Apple Circus. **Opposite page:** James Leonard Joy's set for *Greetings from Coney Island*.

*P*utting on the Show

When you attend a show of the Big Apple Circus, you interact with cashiers, ticket takers, "candy butchers"; (concessionaires), and ushers. You enjoy the daring and artistry of 30 to 40 world-class performers who dispense their magic supported by musicians, a performance director, ring and electrical crews, and follow-spot and sound-board operators. If you know where to look, all of them are visible to you. This is the public face of the Big Apple Circus.

What you do not see is the world behind the curtain. Invisible are the dozens and dozens of people who help put on an amazing show day in and day out. They not only maintain the day-to-day operations of the show on tour, they assist in the unique group effort that is creating a brand-new Big Apple Circus production every year.

Approximately 150 people on the circus payroll travel with the show. The majority of these perform crucial tasks backstage, including the tent crew, grooms, wardrobe staff, administrative staff, cooks, and so on. But this is not all of the organization. About 30 people keep vital departments working at the Big Apple Circus' executive office on Eighth Avenue in Manhattan: Finance, Marketing, Press and Communications, and Development. Eighth Avenue also houses the hub for the Circus' all-important Health and Community Programs, which oversees a national staff of over 100 hospital performers and circus instructors. Unseen, too, is the centralized ticket sales office in Walden, New York, home to the Big Apple Circus' Slifka Family Creative Center, where each year a new show is born.

In 1994, the Big Apple Circus came to Walden and established what is known in the circus world as "winter quarters". In the case of the Big Apple Circus, the right term actually would be "summer quarters". This is where the Circus' equipment is stored between seasons, and also where each new production comes to life during an intensive, six-week rehearsal period. The Circus' veterans love the bucolic village of Walden, remembering only too well when new shows were put together in a makeshift facility at Brooklyn's Floyd Bennett Field. The NYPD helicopters were also based at Floyd Bennett Field, and it was not easy to keep rehearsals focused with the roar of choppers in the background. Besides, an old aviation hangar and runways baked by the summer sun do not make for an ideal creative retreat.

The present rehearsal facility, the Slifka Family Creative Center, was inaugurated in 1997. It covers 30 acres of land and includes a 18,250 square-foot rehearsal space; 37,500 square feet of maintenance shops and storage space; a wing for the production and ticket-sales offices; stables for Katja Schumann's horses; and a residential area for 60 sleeping trailers and caravans. There, each summer, rehearsals for a new show start about August 15th and end with the Big Apple Circus' traditional opening at Dulles Town Center in Virginia, sometime around the 20th of September. It is the final stretch of a long creative process that began two years earlier.

The seeds of a show

Creating a new show is no small affair. It involves a lot of time, patience, imagination, and the creative energies of many individuals whom the audience never sees. And it involves money, of course — never enough of it!

Photo: Maike Schulz

Photo: Theo O. Krath

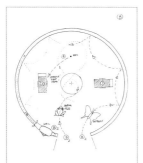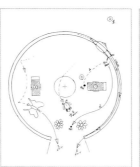

So, to take it as an example of a typical Big Apple Circus show, how was the 25th anniversary production, *Dreams of a City*, created?

The process began in the early fall of 2000 when Paul Binder and Michael Christensen began to bounce back and forth ideas for a new production, the one that was slated to open in two years. The first question they discussed was, what would the show be about? Circus, of course but in which context? A period of time? A place? A story? A character? In short, what would be the theme around which the Big Apple Circus' Creative Team would build a visual, and musical, unity?

Ideas for Big Apple Circus shows often arrive from unexpected places. Set in New York City during the Roaring Twenties, *Jazzmatazz* came to be because the circus' artistic office had spotted the Rizhkov Trio, a group of excellent Russian trapeze artists whose act illustrated that period. The rest of the show developed around that single original image. Paul Binder's childhood memories and a visit to the old B & B Carousell in Coney Island led to *Greetings from Coney Island*, which was set in the early 1900s at the legendary amusement resort (Paul's memories did not go back quite that far). The theme for *Grandma Goes West* was chosen because the previous show had involved 25 Chinese acrobats, and the best way to do something radically different was to do an all-American show.

The theme of *20 Years* was quite obvious; it simply celebrated the 20th anniversary of the Big Apple Circus. For the 25th anniversary production, the initial concept was a similar no-theme, or more accurately, circus-theme idea: In a tribute to the Big Apple Circus' roots, Paul and Michael decided to base the show around a classical equestrian circus at the turn of the twentieth century. But then came September 11, 2001. Although the show's major acts had already been settled upon, it was decided to transform the 25th anniversary production into a tribute to the unflappable spirit of New York. While keeping its classical circus imagery, it became *Dreams of a City*.

Pieces of the puzzle

Jump back to October of 2000. When *Big Top Doo-Wop*, the show that preceded it, was entering its pre-production phase, and right after the opening of *Clown Around Town*, a talent search began for this 25th anniversary production. Artistic Director Paul Binder, Associate Artistic Director Dominique Jando, and General Manager Guillaume Dufresnoy traveled to the circus festivals of Paris and Monte Carlo, visited circuses here and abroad, and reviewed dozens of videotapes. Paul placed telephone calls all over the world to secure the best available artists whose acts could fit into the production's classical equestrian circus theme. Meanwhile, the team researched the time period and gathered books and iconography. Then Creative Director Michael Christensen and the show's guest director, Montreal-based Michel Barette, started working on a script.

Top: Staging diagram for the dream sequence in *The Medicine Show*. Opposite pages: Top: Director Michel Barette (wearing a crown!) shows a movement to (l. To r.) Ivan Vlasov, Valdis Yanovskis, Julian Stachowski, and Regina Dobrovitskaya (*Bello & Friends*). Bottom: Paul directs Elizabeth Griffith and Melinda Merlier in *Jazzmatazz*.

Photo: Maike Schulz

Top: Trying on a circus costume is not always an easy task... Bottom left: In the wardrobe trailer, final touches are applied to a costume shortly before dress rehearsal. Bottom right: Costume designer David Belugou tries a new costume on Katherine Schumann Binder (Jazzmatazz). Opposite page: A costume sketch by Donna Zakowska for Goin' Places.

A production meeting decided the running order of the acts, taking into consideration the rhythms and strengths of each, as well as their technical requirements and the impact they could have on the other acts' needs. The script then laid out the opening sequence's contents and staging, the order of the acts, where the clowns fit in, the contents and staging of the production numbers, as well as directions regarding costuming, lighting, music, etc., etc. In the Creative Team, Dominique Jando was the writer and custodian of the script.

In October of 2001, a first draft of this script was submitted to Paul Binder shortly after the opening of *Big Top Doo-Wop*. Once the draft was accepted, a production meeting was called in which the details were discussed at length. Does the show seem too long or too short? Is this or that idea technically feasible? Does the show order really work? Do the clowns need to create a piece (called a 'reprise') to cover a potentially lengthy ring change? New ideas often emerge from these meetings, which lead to updated versions of the script. Some 20 amended script versions were thus produced during the creative and pre-production periods.

Michael Christensen and Michel Barette went back to the drawing board. Finally, in early 2002, the show was considered ready to be introduced to the set, costume, lighting, and sound designers, as well as the musical director, choreographer, clowning director, and performance director. This first pre-production meeting led to a cascade of new ideas, which bounced back and forth from one participant to another, spawning yet more ideas. The script was amended yet again.

By February, the production's concept reached its final form, and the show was presented to the executive office personnel at Eighth Avenue. Now the show needed a name beyond the working title of *25th Show*. First it became *Little Old New York*, but the marketing and advertising people were not comfortable with that title. After much brainstorming, the list of possible titles was reduced to one: *Dreams of a City*. While the Marketing department began putting together a campaign for *Dreams of a City*, finalized contracts were sent to the performers. They were also told of the various parts they would play according to Michael and Michel's script, which was now set in stone -- for the time being.

A last pre-production meeting was held in June of 2002. Scenic designer Dan Kuchar and costume designer Mirena Rada presented their final sketches; Louis Morisset, the lighting designer, and Darby Smotherman, the sound designer, submitted their technical requirements; Musical Director Rob Slowik and composers Michael Valenti and Scott Sena played the tunes they had written to support the various acts and production numbers. Technical problems were worked out and decisions made, each

Photos: Theo O. Krath

Photos: Theo O. Krath

Top: Company members Yvonne Larson, Eli Milcheva, James Clowney, Melinda Merlier, Julian Stachowski and Carlos Guity rehearse their juggling act for *Grandma Meets Mummenschanz*. Center: A short problem-solving pause during rehearsals of *Grandma Meets Mummenschanz*.: (l. to r.) Paul and performance director Tom Larson (seated), choreographer Lisa Giobbi, lighting designer Jan Kroeze, and acrobatic trainer Lucio Nicolodi working with James Clowney, Carlos Guity, and Melinda Merlier. Bottom: Eli Milcheva and Vesta Geschkova practice in the empty ring (*Carnevale in Venice*).

with close attention to the production budget. This was prepared by General Manager Guillaume Dufresnoy, and kept updated by Tom Larson, acting as production manager, and Production Coordinator Larry Sterner.

Costume construction began in various New York City workshops. (For some productions, costume parts have been made abroad -- in Paris, for instance, where the finest embroiderers can be found). As soon as the tour of *Big Top Doo-Wop* ended, craftsmen and artists began work on the scenic elements, some at the Circus' own shop up in Walden.

The show comes together

By mid-August of 2002, all of these pieces began to assemble at Walden, New York. From all over the world came Russian aerialists, a Swiss juggler, Swedish equestrians, a French clown, a Chinese wire-dancer, an Azerbaijani free-ladder balancer, Pomeranian dogs, Russian cats, a Canadian director, a Rumanian designer, and Bulgarian, Russian, and French acrobats. Among this crowd were a fair number of Americans as well, including musicians, arrangers, and composers. The Slifka Creative Center became a village of its own -- a sort of suburban Tower of Babel.

Members of the resident Company had arrived a little earlier to focus on newly created company acts. They worked with Michel Barette and choreographer Lisa LeAnn Dalton on the production numbers; the guest artists would later be included in some of these. Aerialists were also among the early arrivals, because Performance Director Tom Larson and Ring Crew chief David Gaona needed to figure out the intricate rigging of their aerial equipment and try to solve the problems while time was still easily manageable. And then, Cong Tian, the Chinese wire walker, had problems getting his visa. He arrived just in time to begin rehearsals.

During their first week, guest artists had to adapt to new surroundings, get into new routines, and learn the unfamiliar rules and idiosyncracies of this new circus, which would be their home for the next 10 months. They traveled to Manhattan for costume fittings, while those working for the first time in the United States also experienced the thrill of visiting the local Social Security office. Some of them had to learn a new language; much more adaptable, children often become their parents' translators.

By the beginning of the second week of rehearsals, every part of the Creative Center was bustling with activity. One of the two Big Apple Circus' photographers, Maike Schulz (the other is Bertrand Guay), was taking portraits for the show's souvenir book, as well as candid shots of the rehearsals. Meanwhile, the maintenance crew repaired and repainted everything, including the seating system, the Big Top, and the Circus' 20 caravans; 27 trucks, pick-ups, vans, and motor-homes; and 35 semi-trailers and 12 utility trailers. Music soared from the rehearsal space. In the Big Top, electricians focused the 252 lights used in the show, and Louis Morisset programmed hundreds of lighting cues.

One by one, acts started getting familiar with their new music and their new costumes. Some outfits had to be modified, generally because they did not allow enough freedom of movement, or because some parts had not been built solidly enough. And then came the lighting, which is always difficult in a circus. Not only must the audience be able to view the show, but the acrobats, aerialists, jugglers, and animal trainers need to see perfectly what they are doing. A wrongly positioned light could momentarily blind them and be potentially dangerous. At the same time, the lighting designer still had to create the specific theatrical atmosphere required for each moment of the show.

After the links between each act were worked out, segments of the show were run through over and over, first just with music, then with lighting, and then with costumes. Not surprisingly, problems arose each time an element was added, and they had to be addressed. During the last week, each half of the show was run through several times in front of everybody concerned. After each run-through, an outpouring of notes was given to the cast, technicians, ring crew, costume mistress, and anyone who could help solve the many problems encountered.

Finally, on September 17th, 2002, a full dress rehearsal was presented to a live audience that included the circus' staff, board of directors, various guests, and the villagers of Walden. This was another moment of truth, a decisive stage in the preparation of the show. Before the first real audience, it told the Creative Team what worked and what did not. Notes were given right after the performance, and a last meeting of the Creative Team was held. Necessary cuts, show order changes, and alterations were made, at least on paper, pending the short series of run- throughs at Dulles Town Center just prior to the show's final dress rehearsal. Some of the decisions taken at that moment can be drastic: In *Grandma Goes West*, a saloon brawl involving a dozen performers, as many costumes, and expensive props was cut from the show after only three performances. Despite several revision, the scene never jelled.

If everything goes well, the show has found its final shape by opening night. *Dreams of a City* was no exception -- although the Creative Team was still watching, still taking notes. Michel Barette remained on hand for the five initial performances to make late adjustments. Then the show was finally handed over to Paul, who would be its custodian until the end of the season, still correcting imperfections, taking care of unexpected artistic problems, and making sure that at every performance, the show would be as good as new.

Amazingly, by the end of the first weekend in Dulles Town Center, just before their first break in more than a month, all the artists, musicians, technicians, and crew seemed to have settled into an old, familiar routine. They were also exhausted. But there is nothing more rewarding than hearing the laughter, the "Oohs" and "Aahs" and applause of a happy, revitalized audience. For, as John Steinbeck once put it, "Every man, woman and child comes from the circus refreshed and renewed and ready to survive."

$\mathcal{L}$ife on the Road

Life on the road with the Big Apple Circus is less a journey than a migration. Rather than a trip with a beginning and an end, our village moves with us wherever we go. Our home address ranges from the exclusive enclave of Manhattan's Upper West Side to a farmer's field in rural New Hampshire. No matter where we might be, daily life revolves around the circus. The never-ending demands of the show require that someone be available to handle any emergency, not just at performance times, but around the clock, 365 days a year. Our work is our life, an all-consuming passion that both protects and confines us, day in and day out.

People come and go, bringing with them their unique talents, cultures and sensibilities. The community adapts and changes with each arrival and departure. One thing remains constant, the power of the ring, the unifying element that defines our relationship to one another. For many, the reputation and the quality of the Big Apple Circus is the reason that they come here; for others, the show is an escape from the outside world. They come in search of adventure, excitement or companionship. Once here, they quickly learn that they must make a commitment to this community. Each member of the traveling company plays a role in the larger scheme of things. We simultaneously support and depend upon one another

Circus life is not easy, nor is it forgiving of error. Some people adapt quickly, others will never be comfortable in this environment. Join me for a week on the road to see what you think.

Sunday

There are two shows today, both full houses. The maintenance department is up at dawn to meet local contractors who will service the portable restrooms and haul away yesterday's trash that has been collected in the dumpsters that the purchasing department ordered before we arrived. The uniforms that the staff wore yesterday are laundered beginning at 6 am so that they will be ready when the crew comes to work before the first show. The cooks start breakfast at 7 am. They will serve eggs to order, hash browns and bacon, with lots of hot coffee, beginning at 7:30. Father Jerry Hogan, the national circus chaplain, is in town today. He will set up his "church" in the reception tent so that he can celebrate mass at 9 am. Chairs gathered from the boxes are lined up in front of his temporary altar, a table borrowed from the novelty stand. Missives are passed out to the attendees and the service begins as concessionaires quietly work around the "congregation" of circus folks attending. The intoxicating smell of freshly popped corn and sugary cotton candy drifts across the congregation as the service progresses.

We will move tonight to a new town, so work has already begun to prepare for the jump. Exterior lighting was packed away after the crowd left following last night's performance. The mechanics are making their rounds, checking to ensure that all of the show vehicles are fueled and serviced. Supplies and equipment not required during the day will be stored and secured for the move. Soon after the second show begins, an advance party of several people departs for the new town. They will ensure

Photo: Michael LeClaire

Top: The Big Apple Circus in Philadelphia, right in front of the Art Museum (1987). **Above:** The Big Apple Circus in more bucolic surroundings: Stone Mountain Park, near Atlanta, Georgia (2002). **Opposite page:** William Woodcock and Amy leave the tent after their turn.

Top: Work never stops in the maintenance trailer. Middle: Even the relatively simple task of bringing soil into the ring can generate unexpected problems! Bottom: Putting up the Big Top, however mechanized the operation might be, is always a demanding work. Opposite page: Top: Katja Schumann shares breakfast with her horses. Bottom: A group of performing pigs get a taxi ride to the ring.

that everything is ready at the new location and will be standing by to receive trucks, trailers and RV's as they roll in. After intermission of the second show, the concessions department begins cleaning the food wagons and securing the equipment inside them for the move. The tent crew quietly drops the marquee tent while the show is in progress. Offices and shop wagons are closed up; computers, printers and fax machines are packed away into sturdy road cases; temporary phone lines are cut and commercial truck drivers arrive on the lot to hook up their tractors to the show's semi trailers. The box office closes and the staff totals receipts and prepares reports. When the patrons exit the tent at the end of the show, the midway will have been cleared of extra equipment, most of it already loaded onto trucks in preparation for the move. Even as the band is playing the exit music, crews are busy backstage packing props, loading costumes and dropping sidewall.

The tempo really picks up now as the "load out" begins in earnest. Everyone in the traveling company has an assignment. In a carefully choreographed sequence, work accelerates in every department. Artists and musicians carefully pack props, rigging and instruments. The wardrobe department separates costumes that require dry cleaning from those that will be hand washed. The dry cleaning will be sent to a local cleaner in the next town, with instructions to have it ready prior to the first show. Concessionaires and ushers, having completed their duties in their departments, report to the tent department where they are assigned duties dismantling the seating system or dropping the tent. Electricians begin disconnecting the miles of wiring and cables necessary to power the show. Temporary laborers arrive to augment the traveling crew.

The animal departments are the first to leave the lot. During the show, animal transports were prepared with fresh bedding and feed. As the performing animals complete their work in the ring, they are moved into their traveling accommodations so that stables and animal tents can be dismantled and loaded for the journey. As soon as a path can be cleared, the animals, their trainers and grooms will be on their way to the next town.

Work continues through the night to disassemble not only the big top and its contents, but also the traveling village that surrounds it. Every component of the vast enterprise must be protected, packed away and accounted for before the move. As the various departments complete their work, weary laborers are sent back to their quarters to catch a few minutes of sleep.

Monday

The Big Apple Circus does not move as a caravan down the road; instead, all of the units are given directions to follow and a timeframe for their arrival in the new town. Vehicles depart the old lot throughout the day, traveling at their own pace, making stops as necessary along the way. Generally, the first groups of show semi-trailers are dispatched as they are loaded during tear-down night. Privately owned travel trailers start on their way the next morning, right after dawn, moving out from the old lot and onto the highway as the drivers are ready to move. Show-owned travel trailers leave later in the day.

The crew is roused from sleep early in the morning and sent to work completing whatever tasks remain to be done on the old lot. The sleepers, dormitory trailers housing the majority of the labor force, are sent down the road as soon as everyone has gone to work. Their residents will travel to the next town in passenger vans at the end of the workday.

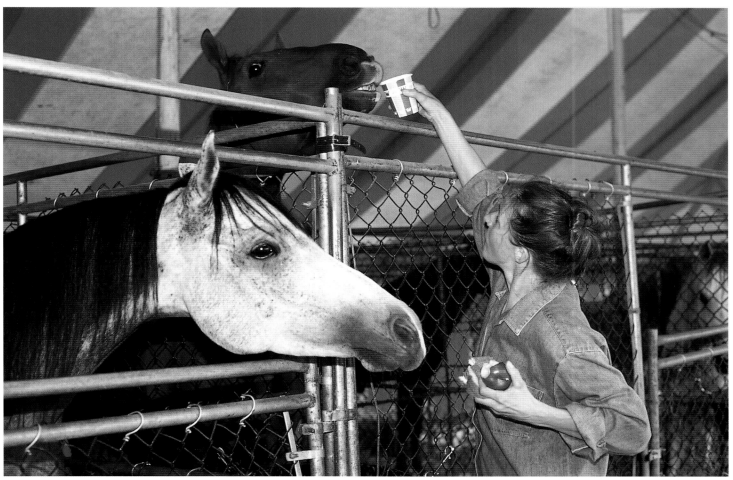

Travel between towns is one of the joys of this lifestyle. No matter how many times you set out on the trip between towns, there is always a sense of excitement as you reach the open road. Memories of past journeys, hopes for the future and a taste of the unknown all combine as you set out on your way. Driving a truck with your home tagging along behind you is far from an easy jaunt down the road. You must constantly be alert for other drivers who don't understand how prudent it would be to provide generous amounts of space between their vehicle and yours. You also cannot zip into any service station or restaurant, but must locate areas that can accommodate your rig. Nonetheless, there is the compensation of watching the countryside glide along outside your window and of discovering the diversity and variety of this great country from its major highways and country roads. It's always a treat, as well, to spot another show vehicle and to wave to the driver as you pass them on the way. If you happen to stop at a highway rest area or service plaza, chances are good that someone else from the show will be there as well, offering you a chance to compare notes on weather, traffic and events along the way.

Upon arrival at the new location, you are met by the advance crew and directed to the spot that will become your home for the length of the stand. The operations department has painstakingly planned the placement of each piece of equipment on the new lot. A computer-aided design program allows them to determine precisely how much space is needed for everything carried by the show. This plan is then used to determine how best to provide electrical power and water as well as access for emergency and service vehicles. The advance crew has marked reference points on the ground that they now use to maneuver things into place. RV residents immediately unhook from tow vehicles as they arrive. The trucks will be moved to a parking

area as quickly as possible to make room for the next wave of arrivals. This first night on a new lot is always exciting. Once settled, everyone takes a stroll around the lot to see where important landmarks are located; the cookhouse, the various offices, the front gate. Newcomers will ask veterans where the nearest grocery store is located or how to get to the post office or the bank. It may be a while before water and power are available, so folks congregate outside enjoying the stars, chatting about the trip, perhaps enjoying a barbeque. It is a good night to turn in early. There is a lot to be done tomorrow.

Tuesday

Work call is early today. The clock is already ticking toward opening night. The majority of the workforce is assigned to the tentmaster. The big top stakes are already in place; the advance crew drove all of them prior to our arrival. Two complete sets of stakes allow us to "leapfrog" from one site to the next. Having the stakes pre-positioned in the ground at the new location saves us the time it would take to wait for stakes to be removed from the old lot, transported here and then driven, one by one into position. The tent crew begins by raising the four masts that will support the tent. It is critical that they are stabilized and guyed out precisely prior to the next phase. It will take three hours for the Big Top to be unrolled from the flatbed trailer that carries it, for the vinyl sections to be laced together and finally for the structure to be raised into position. The side poles are inserted around the exterior in a flurry of activity that is easily the most dramatic moment in the long process.

Simultaneously, in various corners of the lot, animals are being fed and groomed, telephone lines are being strung, offices are being unpacked, rigging and props are being unloaded and decorative and security fencing is being installed. The three cooks in the show's cookhouse are hard at work preparing meals for the workers and staff. They will prepare 150 meals, three times a day throughout the tour. The cookhouse is not only the restaurant, but also the social center of the circus. Everyone passes through there at least once a day. The bulletin board posts helpful information, job openings, personal messages and press clippings. Hot coffee is available around the clock as are soft drinks, milk and water. It is the place to relax, escape the weather, hold impromptu meetings, read the newspaper, play a board game, meet your friends or discuss the world situation.

After lunch, the crew turns their attention to the seating system. Hundreds of pieces need to be assembled in a precise order to construct the seats from which the audience will see the show. The task will require at least twelve hours of dedicated labor. Coincident with the erection of the seats, the electricians must pull hundreds of feet of cable into position. The cables snake from the show's portable generators to the computerized lighting and sound control panels and then to spotlights, moving lights, speakers, props and scenery. The electric crew will spend the rest of the day connecting, checking and focusing all of the lights used in the show. Outside of the Big Top, every RV, office trailer and concessions wagon also requires power. In addition, lights need to be rigged on the exterior of the tent, the box office and the midway.

Left The latest VSO tent setup (2001). **Opposite page:** The old Canobbio tent setup (1990)

Wednesday

It is interesting how quickly things begin to look normal after the move. The ring has been installed in the big top. Two dump-truck loads of sand and clay have been placed in the ring. The dirt, mixed with sawdust, will form the surface of the ring. Horses are brought into the ring to exercise even as work continues around them on the seats, lights and sound. Aerialists hang their rigging and carefully safety check every inch. Offices are operating; telephone, fax and modem lines are in place and working. The box office is open for business.

School opens today in the One-Ring School House, a fully accredited traveling school staffed by three teachers whose only duties are to educate the children traveling with the show. A dedicated semi-trailer is configured with desks, study carrels, computers, blackboards and a library. Students, ranging from elementary to high school age, follow a curriculum that ensures they maintain pace with their contemporaries in New York schools. Classes are held Wednesday through Sunday to coincide with performing schedules. Performing children adjust their school schedules to allow them to dart in and out of class in order to catch their cues in the tent. The teachers have become very adept at utilizing local historic and educational attractions to augment classroom study, another advantage of life on the road.

Delivery trucks roll up to the lot with an amazing assortment of consumable items. The cookhouse and concessions departments receive foodstuffs, for instance, and novelty items need to be replenished as they are sold. Other requirements include feed and bedding for the animals, as well as diesel fuel for generators, air conditioning units and heaters. Show offices replenish their stock of stationery, copy paper, pens, pads and forms. In addition, there is always a need for spare parts for trucks, trailers and RV's. Some of the more esoteric supplies arrive sporadically, but are just as vital… spangles for wardrobe, swivels for aerial rigging, confetti, feathers, clown noses.

We should receive mail today for the first time since moving to the new town. Everyone's mailing address is the show's home office in Manhattan. There, the mailroom collects and forwards postings to wherever the circus may be located. You quickly learn that it pays to calculate how long mail will take to arrive. There is a great value in having automatic payment plans for regular expenses. By doing that, you do not have to worry about possible delays in receiving bills or the time it takes to respond to them.

Thursday

Photos: Bob Tomer

It is opening day in a new town; that means the local inspectors will be visiting this morning to confirm that the circus complies with all regulations for the municipality. The General Manager's office applied for necessary permits several months prior to our arrival and we have already installed whatever we need to bring us up to code. No two places that we visit are exactly the same, so keeping up with each city's statutes is a time consuming, but necessary, part of life on the road. In the afternoon, the concessions department begins to prepare for opening night. The novelty stand is restocked with supplies. After the food wagons are scrubbed from top to bottom, food and drink preparations begin. The show's restaurant-size freezer has been manufacturing and storing ice cubes since we arrived. Now, coolers are filled with the ice,

The One Ring School House

It's nine o'clock Saturday morning and the children of the Big Apple Circus are heading to school. Saturday and Sunday are just normal school days for us. We have Monday and Tuesday as our "weekend".

School lasts from nine to twelve in the morning for the high school students and one middle school student, and from one to four in the afternoon for the elementary students. Two teachers rotate days tutoring the older class, one day for math and science, another for history and literature. The younger students have one permanent teacher every day for all of their subjects.

Our school is housed in a large white semi-truck, painted with bright stars and the circus' logo. Inside, our classroom is divided into three areas, one for the younger class, one for the older class, and one room housing the library, an extensive collection of books for all ages and interests. We each have our own cubby for work and keeping our tex books and supplies, but some students much prefer to work on the beanbag- and pillow-covered floor of the library. We have three computers available for our use, two connected to the Internet and ready for exploration and research. Each week, some of us in the high school group study foreign languages with local teachers from the area. We have special one-on-one sessions in either French or Spanish with the tutor.

Every town that we visit on the circus tour holds many possibilities for field trips and excursions. Museums, historical sites and interesting attractions are readily visited during our stay in each area.

We circus children receive a very personalized education; we're able to learn at our own levels and speeds. Our teachers know where every student needs help and where they are strong. Each one of us gets an education based on our special needs and goals. We are all getting a diverse and very unique learning experience that will influence us throughout our lives.

Anne Covington
10th Grade Student

What an incredible experience! To be a teacher in the One-Ring School House is such a unique and rewarding educational opportunity. From hiking up Stone Mountain in Georgia to walking the Freedom Trail in Boston, the world is our classroom. I feel quite fortunate to be able to travel throughout this country and teach at the same time. It is a dream come true. However, the best part of this adventure is working with the students. To teach students of all ages with diverse cultural backgrounds is both fascinating and challenging. What an education!

Karen Scott
Teacher, One-Ring School House, 2000-2002

Photo: Holton Rower

Photo: Bertrand Guay

Every year, Paul Newman hosts a benefit performance for the Scott Newman Foundation at the Big Apple Circus. One year, he decided to perform as a clown along with Michael Christensen. When he was finished, he needed a place to remove his makeup, so I volunteered my trailer. He used one of my small towels to remove his clown makeup, and naturally the towel was covered with makeup. But it wasn't just anyone's makeup, it was Paul Newman's makeup. Now each year the clowns and crew would hold a benefit performance to raise funds for our own school, the One Ring Schoolhouse. So a plan was hatched that day to auction off what was billed as "The Newman Towel." With a prestigious New York law firm's affidavit declaring its authenticity and a signed letter from Mr. Newman, two security guards accompanied me and this dirty towel to the auction, which was held in our ring. After the auctioneer, Michael Christensen, read the letter of authenticity, the bidding quickly soared. Thanks to the generosity and wonderful sense of humor of one of our great supporters, "The Newman Towel" raised $2000 for the One Ring Schoolhouse.

Barry Lubin

Top: Idyllic family life on the road: Karyn and Michael Christensen (as Mr. Stubs) with their daughters Kyla and Ivy. **Middle:** A group of eager students pose in front of the first "Little Red One-Ring School House." **Bottom:** The new, state-of-the-art schoolhouse-on-wheels today. **Opposite page:** Max Binder and his dog, Scruffy, wait for their turn in the ring (*Jazzmatazz*).

Photo: Theo O. Krath

Photos: Holton Rower

Top left: Backstage, just before the start of the show (*Jazzmatazz*). Top right: Delilah and Barbara Woodcock wait for their turn. Middle: Sacha Pavlata, Marie-Pierre Benac, and David Dimitri warm up before their act. Bottom: Jim Tinsman practices his hand-balancing on the "back lot."

some of which is sent to the snow cone machine where it is finely crushed, while the rest goes into freezers in the food wagons to be used for cold drinks. Bags of sugar are spun into cotton candy. Each bouquet is hand made, then wrapped in plastic and placed on the boards that the concessionaires will use to transport it into the tent. Just prior to show time, the aroma of freshly popped corn drifts over the lot. There is no better indicator that it is time for performances to begin.

In the big top, the house crew has been busy mopping the floorboards and wiping down each seat in the stands. The ring crew has rolled out the heavy ring carpet and placed it into position in the center of the ring. The sawdust and dirt around it are then meticulously raked smooth. Technicians check every lighting cue. The band assembles on the bandstand and runs through several tunes to allow the sound technician to confirm settings.

Backstage, the first of the artists are warming up. Each one has their own ritual of stretching, balancing and rehearsing for their work in the ring. Like any athlete, they understand the importance of conditioning and take every precaution to ensure that they are prepared for the exacting work ahead. The wardrobe department has checked each of the costumes, repairing any damage, then lays them out in the wardrobe truck in the order they will be used. Clown Alley, tucked into a corner of the backstage area of the tent, is a colorful confusion of costumes, props and makeup. A little over an hour before the first scheduled show, a calm descends on the lot. All of the advance preparations are complete. The audience has not yet begun to arrive so the artists and staff have a moment to relax, to collect their thoughts and to move into "show mode". The quiet does not last long, however as the call of "doors" reminds everyone that it is time to show a select group of customers what we can do. After a briefing by the house manager, the ushers move to their assigned positions. The ticket takers swing open the gates of the marquee tent and the public enters the front yard.   Our life will be regulated by the show schedule from now until we move on to the next town. Everyone understands what they must do and when it will happen relative to show times. Practically the entire traveling company is involved in the performance. Even those whose duties at first seem removed, must adjust their work to ensure that what they are doing does not conflict with the show.

The band becomes your "alarm clock" during the show. Rather than look at your watch, you automatically listen to the music coming from the tent. Once you learn the cues, it is obvious when an act is running long, or that something has been shortened,

Photo: Holton Rower

Photo:Theo O. Krath

just by hearing what the band is doing. People will ask you, "What's on?" and you can say "horses" or "the flying act" after only a few seconds of listening. The artists become so proficient at this skill that they can relax backstage until the last second before a cue, confident that the music coming from the bandstand will let them know exactly how much time they have until their entrance.

The local critics will attend tonight's show. It's always interesting to see what they think of our production, though the comments of the customers leaving the tent are just as telling. You can stand by the exit and catch a word or phrase from people as they pass by. It makes your day when you hear: "That is the best circus I have ever seen".

Now that we are settled into place, there will be time for community activities. The barbecues come out after the end of the show. People gather in groups to enjoy ethnic treats from around the world. If anyone has had a birthday recently, there will be parties, gift exchanges and celebrations. National days, from Cinco de Mayo to Bastille Day to the Fourth of July, are big events, always worthy of celebration, even if they have to be shifted slightly to accommodate the show schedule.

Photos: Holton Rower

Friday

Top left: Bert Lubin just enjoyed her performance. **Top right:** Carlos Guity, Melinda Merlier wait backstage (*Jazzmatazz*). **Middle:** While the show is going on, Grandma (Barry Lubin) pays a visit to the concession stand. **Bottom:** The tent and the ring are being outfitted for the next series of performances.

It is payday, a highlight of everyone's calendar. Paychecks are distributed first thing in the morning to each of the departments. Supervisors then pass them out to their subordinates. The amount that you receive in your paycheck often varies from one pay period to the next. Each of the states in which we play has its own rules for withholding payroll taxes. The finance department adjusts pay accordingly. Therefore, the amount of pay you take home is determined by the state in which you last worked. The purchasing department will take one of the show vans to a neighborhood bank this morning. The tellers there have been authorized to cash Big Apple Circus checks for anyone who has a valid circus photo ID card. There will be a stop at a local grocery store on the way back to the lot, offering a chance to restock essential supplies before reporting to work for the first show.

A gentle rain has begun to fall. The old axiom, "the show must go on", certainly applies in the circus business. We have had performances in snow, rain, mud and blazing heat. The audience is comfortable inside the big top, where the environment is

Photos: Patricia Lanza

Photo: Don Covington

Top: The Big Apple Circus in Boston. **Bottom:** The circus on the road during the early 1980's, with its first Italian-made Big Top. **Opposite page:** Putting the final touch on the tent, atop one of the masts.

Previous pages, **Top left:** The audience arrives (1983). **Bottom left:** Rik Albani and his musicians get ready for the show. **Top right** The concession stands are always busy before the show. **Bottom right:** The Big Top in Reston, Virginia.

controlled with air conditioning or heaters, while the artists and staff must survive with the elements outside. Although umbrellas and ponchos cover uniforms and wardrobe, and tarps provide protection for props and scenery, the transit between one spot and the next can become an adventure. Temporary dikes divert water away from the tents; electrical cables and connections are elevated to clear raceways for water run-off. Wooden planks form walkways over muddy spots and sump pumps drain water from low places as necessary. Despite the inconvenience, there are compensations. The acoustics in the big top improve when the vinyl is wet; the band can sound like a 20 piece orchestra when the conditions are right and there is no better way to fall asleep than while hearing the patter of rain on the roof of your trailer.

The circus kids polish their skills in the ring whenever they can find time. Parents carefully tutor their children from the time that they begin to walk. Riding a unicycle or balancing on one's hands moves from being play to a life's work. Hours and hours of dedicated practice time produce amazing results. Circus kids learn the value of concentration and professionalism early in their lives and carry those skills with them wherever they go. Surrounded by role models who are world-class athletes as well as polished performers, they quickly develop the bearing and presence of seasoned professionals.

Saturday

The majority of the world is settling in to enjoy the weekend. The circus is gearing up for its peak business. There will be at least two and sometimes three shows on a Saturday. Chances are good that every seat will be filled, guaranteeing that all of us will be busy ensuring that the customers are provided the very best experience possible. Circus people realize that every show is important; the customers filing into the tent are anxiously awaiting what we have prepared for them. Unlike those of us who work here, they have never seen the performance. For them, everything is new and exciting. Our job is to keep the experience fresh day after day. Watching the audience entering the big top helps us to do that. The mood is set with their first look at the interior, a mysterious space filled with rigging, lights and the set. Though it affects everyone, children are the most vocal. "Wow!" they exclaim, "Cool!" From that beginning, you build the magic that serves to take the customers away from their lives in the outside world. Our lives will connect with theirs as they experience the circus. When the show ends, they will leave the tent to return to their version of reality, while we, who remain, will glory in ours.

Don Covington

Photo: Holton Rower

Photo:Theo O. Krath

1981-1984

The first of the 21 shows presented so far at Manhattan's Lincoln Center for the Performing Arts was produced by Judith Friedlaender and Ivor David Balding (later the creator of Saint Louis, Missouri-based Circus Flora). The subsequent shows until 1983 were produced by Judith Friedlaender, then the Big Apple Circus' Executive Director. All these productions were conceived and directed by Paul Binder. Michael Christensen was the Producing Clown (a title that became Clown Coordinator in 1983), Rik Albani was the Musical Director, and the Production Manager was Robert Libbon. Jan Kroeze signed the lighting design — a task that had been his since the first Big Apple Circus performance. In 1983, the Big Apple Circus hired its first costume designer, James T. Corry (who stayed aboard until 1985), and the following year composer Linda Hudes started a collaboration with the circus which lasted 13 years.

High-wire dancer Philippe Petit; the Flying Gaonas, featuring the great triple-somersaulter Tito Gaona; the juggler Michael Moschen; Ben Williams and Anna May, Bill Woodcock's star elephant; the Dymeks on the Russian Barre; Danish equestrienne Katja Schumann (who was to become Mrs. Paul Binder); Francis Brunn, a true living legend of the juggling world; the Polish Wozniak Troupe on the teeterboard; the beautiful Dolly Jacobs on the Roman Rings; the Carillo Brothers on the high-wire; Roby Gasser and his amazing sea-lions; Koma Zuru and his spinning tops; and David Dimitri, Sacha Pavlata and Marie-Pierre Benac, among others, were the first international circus stars to grace the Big Apple Circus' ring.

1981

Cast: Philippe Petit ⁂ The Flying Gaonas ⁂ Alexandre (Sacha) Pavlata ⁂ Michael Christensen & Paul Binder ⁂ The Back Street Flyers ⁂ The Bertinis ⁂ Carol Buckley and "Tarra" ⁂ Michael Moschen ⁂ Katja Schumann ⁂ Jim & Tisha Tinsman ⁂ **Ringmaster:** Carlo Pellegrini

1982

Cast: Sacha Pavlata ⁂ David Müller (David Dimitri) ⁂ Jim & Tisha Tinsman ⁂ The Canestrellis ⁂ Ben Williams & "Anna May" ⁂ Katja Schumann ⁂ Koma Zuru - The Back Street Flyers ⁂ Michael & Paul ⁂ The Dymeks ⁂ The Flying Gaonas ⁂ **Ringmaster:** Paul Binder ⁂ **The Big Apple Circus Clowns**: Michael Christensen, Barry Lubin, Carlo Pellegrini, with Jeff Gordon

1983

Cast: Nathalie Enterline ⁂ Luis Muñoz ⁂ Heidi Herriott ⁂ Katja Schumann ⁂ The Wozniak Troupe ⁂ Francis Brunn ⁂ The Back Street Flyers ⁂ Jim Tinsman ⁂ The Woodcock Family ⁂ Michael Christensen & Paul Binder ⁂ Tisha Tinsman ⁂ The Flying Gaonas ⁂ with Sacha Pavlata, Iris Lopez and Andrea Urena ⁂ **Ringmaster**: Paul Binder ⁂ **The Big Apple Circus Clowns**: Michael Christensen, Jeff Gordon, Barry Lubin, Carlo Pellegrini

1984

Cast: James Zoppe & The Big Apple Circus Rosinback Riders ⁂ The Carillo Brothers ⁂ Marie-Pierre Benac ⁂ Sacha Pavlata ⁂ David Dimitri ⁂ Roby Gasser ⁂ Katja Schumann ⁂ Dolly Jacobs ⁂ The Woodcock Family ⁂ Jim Tinsman ⁂ Tisha Tinsman ⁂ The Flying Gaonas ⁂ **Ringmaster**: Paul Binder
The Big Apple Circus Clowns: Michael Christensen, Barry Lubin, Jeff Gordon

Top: Michael and Paul clowning in the first Lincoln Center production. The Ringmaster (left) is Carlo Pellegrini. Far left: The inimitable Michael Moschen with his torches. Left: The Bertinis. Opposite page: Ringmaster Carlo Pellegrini introduces the opening "charivari."

The first reason I go every year to the Big Apple Circus is because it has become a New York institution — and like other great institutions, you keep revisiting.

Secondly, my six-year-old daughter, Talicia, enjoys visiting the Big Apple Circus more than anything. It is her favorite event on her annual calendar.

And third, I am a patriot at heart, and I want to support the endeavors of my fellow Dane, Katja Schumann!

Peter Martins
Ballet Master in Chief
New York City Ballet

63

Photo: A. Gaonoa

In the winter of 1982, I made my debut at Lincoln Center with the Big Apple Circus. Just before the show I decided to wander around the reception tent in full clown makeup dressed as Grandma, just to get a feel for the audience that night. Spotting me, a Lincoln Center security guard asked to see my ticket. I rummaged through my carpet bag and handed him a ticket to a Liberace concert from 1979. He took one look at that and called over an NYPD officer and together they promptly threw me out. Just then, the overture started for my very first show at Lincoln Center, and as much fun as it had been being ejected, I was now starting to panic. Fortunately, also wandering through the reception tent was one of the flying trapeze artists who realized my dilemma. He quickly identified me as one of the clowns, and I was promptly readmitted just in time for what was then the biggest night of my career.

Barry Lubin

Koma Zuru has been designated a "Living National Treasure" by the Japanese government. His act . . .

top spinning!

P.B.

Top: Barry Lubin, not as Grandma, Jeff Gordon, not as Gordoon but as a plant in the audience, Michael as Mr. Stubs, a young "volunteer," and Carlo Pellegrini. **Bottom:** Barry Lubin as Grandma

Opposite page: Top Left: Koma Zuru. **Top right:** Ben Williams and Anna May. **Bottom:** Carlo Pellegrini, Grandma, and Mr. Stubs, the Big Apple Circus's first clown trio.

Photo: Martha Swope Assoc./Linda Alaniz

Photo: Jean-Marie Guyaux

Photo: Jean-Marie Guyaux

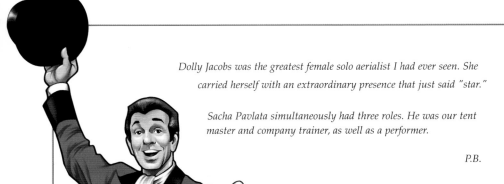

Dolly Jacobs was the greatest female solo aerialist I had ever seen. She carried herself with an extraordinary presence that just said "star."

Sacha Pavlata simultaneously had three roles. He was our tent master and company trainer, as well as a performer.

P.B.

Top: The beautiful Dolly Jacobs, Queen of the Rom. Rings. **Right:** Sacha Pavlata on the Cloud Swing – t ancestor of the trapeze.

_____

Following pages:

Left: Juggling legend Francis Brunn: Juggling fans did hesitate to travel hundreds of miles to see him perfor wherever the Big Apple Circus was! **Right:** A classica trained dancer, Carlo Pellegrini started as the circu Ringmaster, then, for the next two seasons, played t traditional European white-face clown opposite t *augustes* Mr. Stubs and Grandma.

Photo: Jean-Marie Guyaux

Photo: Jean-Marie Guyaux

Top: A Gold Medal winner at the Festival Mondial du Cirque de Demain in Paris, the Spanish acrobat Luis Muñoz performed a rare layout somersault on the tight wire. Right: Nathalie Enterline was a national baton twirling champion who became a protégée of the great juggler Francis Brunn. The result was an astonishing act that won a Gold Medal in the Festival du Cirque de Demain in Paris.

to: Jean-Marie Guyaux

The now legendary clown trio of the Big Apple Circus's early years: **Top:** A tender moment between Mr. Stubs (Michael Christensen) and Grandma (Barry Lubin). **Bottom:** Grandma, Mr. Stubs, and Gordoon (Jeff Gordon) in a spirited rock-and-roll moment. **Opposite page:** Desperately in love, Mr. Stubs offers his heart to the magnificent Dolly Jacobs.

Michael Christensen (Mr. Stubs), Jeff Gordon (Gordoon), and Barry Lubin (Grandma) were a wonderful clown team. We counted on them for original laughs that were stamped with the Big Apple Circus signature.

P.B.

Roby Gasser's sea lion, Adolf, was a natural clown. Critic Clive Barnes observed: "At the end of the act, I fully expected to see a man unzip and climb out of the sea lion suit." The act was another winner of the Gold Clown at the International Circus Festival of Monte Carlo.

Marie-Pierre Benac created, or was partner in 10 different acts over seven years as a Big Apple Circus Company member. She was extraordinary and always gave an effort of 110%.

P.B.

Photo: Martha Swope Assoc./Linda Alaniz

Left: Smiling as always, triple-somersaulter star Tito Gaona swings on the flying trapeze. His brother Richie and sister Chela are on the platform. **Opposite page:** The Big Apple Circus Rosinback Riders: Jens Larson, Sacha Pavlata, and James Zoppe (bottom), with Bert Lubin, Marie-Pierre Benac, and Mafalda Zoppe (on top).

Previous pages

Left: Marie-Pierre Benac on the Russian Barre, with David Dimitri (left) and Sacha Pavlata: three pillars of the original Big Apple Circus Resident Company. **Top right:** Roby Gasser and his wonderful partner, Adolf. **Bottom right:** The Woodcock family provided the Big Apple Circus with original elephant acts from 1982 to 1998. Delilah (on Toto), Barbara, Shannon (standing near the ring entrance), and the legendary William "Buckles" Woodcock (in tuxedo).

Photo: Holton Rower

Top left: Hand-balancer and Company member Jimmy Tinsman piling "bricks" atop of his ladder. **Top right:** James Zoppe performing an extremely difficult pirouette on the back of his cantering horse. **Bottom left:** A young Paul in his traditional role: Ringmaster of the Big Apple Circus.

Opposite page: The Wozniak Troupe in their spectacular Russian Swing act.

1985

The First Circus in America

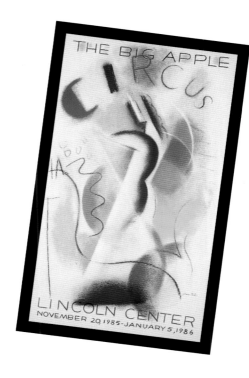

Directed by: **Paul Binder**
Musical Director: **Rik Albani**
Original Music: **Linda Hudes**
Clown Coordinator: **Michael Christensen**
Ring Director: **Robert Libbon**
Costumes: **James T. Corry**
Lighting Design: **Jan Kroeze**
Musical Arrangements: **Linda Hudes & Rik Albani**

Cast: Dolly Jacobs David Dimitri Marie-Pierre Benac Jim Tinsman Dimitri Ben Williams The Wozniak Troupe Sacha Pavlata Katja Schumann **Ringmaster**: Paul Binder **The Big Apple Circus Clowns**: Michael Christensen, Barry Lubin, Jeff Gordon

This was the first Big Apple Circus show conceived around a theme. The great Swiss clown Dimitri was the guest star of the Lincoln Center season, along with the magnificent Dolly Jacobs, returning by popular demand. Katja Schumann became the first woman in America to present a complete version of the nineteenth-century equestrian classic, *The Courier*. The Big Apple Circus' Company was formed, and included David Dimitri (Dimitri's son), Marie-Pierre Benac, Sacha Pavlata, Jim and Tisha Tinsman, and the now-legendary Big Apple Circus clown team of Michael Christensen (Mr. Stubs), Barry Lubin (Grandma), and Jeff Gordon (Gordoon).

Left: The unforgettable smile of a great clown: Dimitri. **Right:** Company members David Dimitri (Dimitri's son) and Marie-Pierre Benac dance on the tight wire.

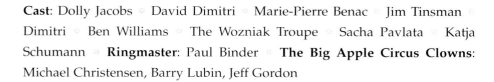

Photo: Lynn Saville

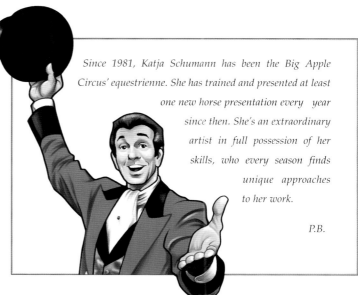

Since 1981, Katja Schumann has been the Big Apple Circus' equestrienne. She has trained and presented at least one new horse presentation every year since then. She's an extraordinary artist in full possession of her skills, who every season finds unique approaches to her work.

P.B.

Top: Katja Schumann performs the nineteenth-century equestrian classic, *The Courier*. Paul is in charge of the horses. **Left:** Company member Jim Tinsman performs his one-arm stand.

Opposite page: Top: Katja Schumann as her usual self: whispering to her horses. **Bottom left:** The Wozniak Troupe in their teeterboard act. Julian Stachowski (bottom right) stayed with the Circus when the troupe broke up. **Bottom right:** Jeff Gordon (Gordoon) in his trademark "TP" routine, which he created at the Big Apple Circus.

1986

Carnivals & Mardi-Gras

Directed by: **Paul Binder**
Musical Director: **Rik Albani**
Original Music: **Linda Hudes**
Clown Coordinator: **Michael Christensen**
Costumes by: **Donna Zakowska**
Lighting design: **Jan Kroeze**
Associate Director: **Dominique Jando**
Ring Director: **Robert Libbon**

Cast: The Dynamotion Jugglers ✿ Tisha Tinsman ✿ David Dimitri ✿ Marie-Pierre Benac ✿ Denis Lacombe ✿ Katja Schumann ✿ Johnny Martin ✿ Lisa & the Trampoline Guys ✿ Bill Woodcock ✿ Jim Tinsman ✿ The Flying Gaonas ✿ **Ringmaster**: Paul Binder ✿ **The Big Apple Circus Clowns**: Michael Christensen, Barry Lubin, Jeff Gordon

Johnny Martin and his wonderfully "lazy" dog Lady were the stars of this Lincoln Center production, along with the uproarious Canadian clown, Denis Lacombe, in his "Maestro" parody. The Venetian Carnevale section, which centered around Katja Schumann's liberty horses, was the most successful moment of the production; in 1993, the idea would be fully developed as *Carnevale in Venice*.

Top: Company member Tisha Tinsman in one of her aerial acts. **Right**: Company members David Dimitri (left) and Jim Tinsman performed an aerial ladder act together. **Opposite page**: **Top**: The late Johnny Martin and his lazy dog, Lady: one of the funniest animal acts of all times. **Bottom**: Another very funny character, Canadian clown Denis Lacombe (left), sings along with Mr. Stubs and Gordoon.

Photos: Martha Swope

Photo: Martha Swope Assoc./ Linda Alaniz

Photo: Martha Swope Assoc./ Linda Alaniz

Left: Mr. Stubs (Michael Christensen) with a smaller version of "Leonard." **Bottom:** The opening of the first Big Apple Circus production built around a theme, *The First Circus in America*, with costumes by James T. Corry.

The first year I performed in the Big Apple Circus, my fellow clowns Michael Christensen, Jeff Gordon and I did an audience participation routine. At each show Ringmaster Paul Binder picked a child from the audience to compete against the clowns. The routine went very well and the child triumphed against the clowns, naturally, and went back to his seat to great applause. The next day we received a note from the mother of the child telling us that her son was autistic and that this was the first time in his life that he truly connected to anything. It was in her words, a breakthrough. She thanked us profusely for choosing her son, and for the effect it had on her and her family watching him perform in the ring that day. After reading the note, the clowns remembered that for those few moments there was nothing unusual or remarkable about the boy, and then we cried for the fact that for those few moments there was nothing unusual or remarkable about the boy.

Barry Lubin

Opposite page: Top: The Dynamotion Jugglers (Jim Strinka and Barrett Felker). **Bottom:** David Dimitri and Marie-Pierre Benac, in a dancing duet on the tight-wire.

1001 Nights at the Big Apple Circus

Directed by: **Paul Binder**
Musical Director: **Rik Albani**
Original Music: **Linda Hudes**
Clown Coordinator: **Michael Christensen**
Costumes by: **Donna Zakowska**
Lighting by: **Jan Kroeze**
Scenic design by: **Nancy Winters**
Associate Director: **Dominique Jando**
Ring Director: **Robert Libbon**

Cast: Lisa Dufresne ☼ Jim Tinsman ☼ Phil Beder ☼ Hugo Zamoratte ☼ Katja Schumann ☼ Jing Xiao Yi & Wang Jing Hua ☼ Les Casaly ☼ The Dancing Gauchos ☼ Marie-Pierre Benac ☼ David Dimitri ☼ Bill Woodcock ☼ Dolly Jacobs ☼ The Tangier Troupe ☼ **Ringmaster**: Paul Binder ☼ **The Big Apple Circus Clowns:** Michael Christensen, Jeff Gordon, David Casey, John Lepiarz

Ten years! The Big Apple Circus had come of age! For the first time, the Circus used the talents of a scenic designer, Nancy Winters, for this show whose Arabian Nights theme was fully integrated into the production. Highlights of the season were the amazing Argentinian contortionist Hugo Zamoratte (the Genie in the Bottle), the Dancing Gauchos (also from Argentina), and for the first time an act from the People's Republic of China. The animal cast included camels and goats. (In the summer, animal presenter Lisa Dufresne was replaced by Bobby Gibbs). Two newcomers made their hilarious debut in Clown Alley, John Lepiarz (Mr. Fish) and David Casey (Oaf). Les Casaly (Guillaume and Mireille Dufresnoy) made their Big Apple Circus debut with their superb aerial casting cradle act. Today, Guillaume Dufresnoy is the Big Apple Circus' General Manager. And a very talented costume designer, Donna Zakowska, started a long collaboration with the Circus.

Right: Mr. Paul, the Ringmaster, tries to make sense of Mr. Stubs and Gordoon's oriental shenanigans. **Opposite page:** A spectacular pyramid by the Tangier Troupe, Moroccan tumblers.

Photo: Martha Swope

Photo: Meryl Joseph

Left: The amazing contortio
Hugo Zamoratte, from Argent
was a former accountant. **Bott**
The wonderful Dancing Gauc
arguably the best sabateo dancer
the business today. **Opposite p**
Gordoon and Oaf (David Cas
prepare to pull a table cloth f
under a not-so-confident "volunte

Following pages

Left: Top: Katja Schumannn and
Arabian horses. **Bottom left:** H
Zamoratte, the "Genie in the Bot
Bottom Right: Guillaume
Mireille Dufresnoy in the ele
aerial cradle act they performec
the Casaly Duo. Today, Guillaum
the Circus' General Manager. **Ri**
David Dimitri and Marie-Pi
Benac in a superb pas-de-deux
William Woodcock's elephants.

Photo: Martha Swope Assoc./Linda Alaniz

Photos: Martha Swope Assoc./Linda Alaniz

Zamoratte was truly unforgettable. People referred to him as "pretzel-man" or "rubberman." He could bend and twist himself and climb into a jar that was two feet in diameter and only three feet high.

P.B.

1988

The Big Apple Circus Meets the Monkey King

Directed by: **Paul Binder**
Musical Director: **Rik Albani**
Original Music: **Linda Hudes**
Clown Coordinator: **Michael Christensen**
Costumes by: **Donna Zakowska**
Lighting by: **Jan Kroeze**
Scenic design by: **Nancy Winters**
Associate Director: **Dominique Jando**
Ring Director: **Robert Libbon**

Cast: The Nanjing Acrobatic Troupe, featuring Yang Xiao Di, Chen Wei Hong, and the Qian Brothers ☆ Katja Schumann ☆ Annie Dugan-Potts ☆ Carol Mark ☆ Jim Tinsman ☆ Meda Crina ☆ Taso Stavrakis ☆ Vanessa Thomas ☆ Robert Libbon ☆ Tisha Tinsman ☆ William Woodcock ☆ Roby Gasser ☆ Les Casaly ☆ **Ringmaster**: Paul Binder ☆ **The Big Apple Circus Clowns**: Michael Christensen, Jeff Gordon, David Casey, John Lepiarz

The stars of this spectacular production were 25 performers from the Nanjing Acrobatic Troupe, led by their artistic director, Lu Yi, one of China's finest circus artists. It was an "East meets West" story whose central characters were the Big Apple Circus Clowns, headed by Michael Christensen (his character, Mr. Stubs, made his last appearance in this Big Apple Circus production), and the Monkey King, a popular character from the Beijing opera tradition (impersonated by the clown-acrobat Yang Xiao Di). And Roby Gasser returned with his beloved sea-lions Adolf and Taxi.

All 1988 Photos: Patricia Lanza

Left: The extraordinary juggling act of the Qian Brothers. **Opposite page:** Thirteen performers on a single bicycle: the Nanjing Acrobatic Troupe.

Top left: Toto, William Woodcock's Asian male elephant. Top right: Roby Gasser and Adolf were back by popular demand. Left: Yang Xiao Di as the Monkey King. Opposite page: Top left: A traditional staple of Chinese acrobatics, the Lion Dance. Top right: The wonderful spinning-plate act of the Nanjing Acrobatic Troupe. Bottom: In the show's opening, the unicorn of the western mythology woke up the Big Apple Circus clowns; in a few moments, they will meet the Chinese Monkey King.

Following pages:

Left: Two graceful members of the Nanjing Acrobatic Troupe spin plates atop of bamboo sticks while balancing head-to-head. Right: Juggling skill contest between the Chinese Monkey King (Yang Xiao Di) and the all-American Mr. Fish (John Lepiarz).

1989

Grandma Goes West

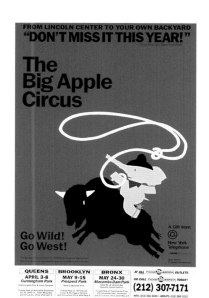

Conceived and directed by: **Paul Binder**
Musical Director: **Rik Albani**
Original Music: **Linda Hudes**
Clown Coordinator: **Michael Christensen**
Costumes by: **Donna Zakowska**
Lighting by: **Jan Kroeze**
Scenic design by: **James Leonard Joy**
Associate Director: **Dominique Jando**
Choreographer: **Monica Lévy**
Production Manager: **Robert Libbon**
Ring Director: **Guillaume Casaly**
Shadow Puppet Design: **Stephen Kaplin**

Cast: Katja Schumann ✷ Jenny Klion ✷ Melinda Merlier ✷ Olivier Merlier ✷ Vanessa Thomas ✷ Pedro Reis ✷ David Rosaire ✷ César ✷ Vince Bruce ✷ Guillaume Casaly ✷ Mireille Casaly ✷ Taso Stavrakis ✷ The Williams Family ✷ The Rios Brothers ✷ The Loyal-Suarez Troupe ✷ **Ringmaster**: Paul Binder The **Big Apple Circus Clowns**: Barry Lubin, David Casey, John Lepiarz

After the exoticism of The Big Apple Circus Meets the Monkey King, it was decided to revert to an all-American theme — the Wild West. The show marked the return of Big Apple Circus' perennial favorite, Grandma. The wonderful Rios Brothers with their Risley act; Vince Bruce, world-champion roper and very funny comedian; and the hilarious clown and mime César headed the cast. The show also featured aerialist Pedro Reis, the Loyal-Suarez equestrian troupe, and the antics of David Rosaire's rambunctious Perky Pekes. On the animal side, the true star was A-Yan-A, the gentle buffalo. Fresh from the Hungarian National Circus School, Melinda and Olivier Merlier (she, Hungarian; he, French) made their debut as resident Company members. Scenic designer James Leonard Joy joined the Circus' Creative Team for the first of several highly successful collaborations.

All 1989 Photos: Patricia Lanza

Top: James Leonard Joy's set for *Grandma Goes West*. **Right**: Aerialist Pedro Reis dressed by Donna Zakowska. **Opposite page**: An audience favorite: David Rosaire's Perky Pekes, with other assorted animals.

César appeared with us twice. He was a mime-comedian who would never let go until the audience was howling with laughter. I think there is nothing more refreshing than hearing 1500 people enjoying a good laugh together.

P.B.

Above: César fighting with his recalcitrant suitcase. **Opposite page:** Mr. Fish (John Lepiarz) successfully roped Oaf (David Casey).

Previous pages: Left page: Timmy Loyal and Magdalena Suarez, of the Loyal-Suarez Troupe. Taso Stavrakis is at the curtain. **Right page, left:** New Company members, Olivier and Melinda Merlier. **Top right:** Pedro Reis on the Cloud Swing. **Middle right:** Grandma feeds a member of the audience... **Bottom right:** The lariat king, and a wonderful comedian, Vince Bruce.

1990

Ballerinas, Horses and Clowns: the Golden Age

Conceived and directed by: **Paul Binder**
Musical Director: **Rik Albani**
Original Music: **Linda Hudes**
Clown Coordinator: **Michael Christensen**
Costumes by: **Donna Zakowska**
Lighting by: **Jan Kroeze**
Scenic design by: **James Leonard Joy**
Associate Director: **Dominique Jando**
Choreographer: **Monica Lévy**
Performance Director: **Guillaume Dufresnoy**
Marionette Design: **Peter Baird**

Cast: Carlos Guity   Susanne Svenson   Carlos Svenson   Taso Stavrakis   Olivier Merlier   Melinda Merlier   Marie-Pierre Benac   Katja Schumann   Annie Dugan   The Alexis Brothers   Vanessa Thomas   David Dimitri   The Williams Family   Al Calienes   The Panteleenko Brothers   **Ringmaster**: Paul Binder   **The Big Apple Circus Clowns**: Barry Lubin, David Casey, John Lepiarz

In this very successful, beautifully dressed production, the Big Apple Circus paid homage to its roots: the classical circus of Victorian Europe. The stars of the show were the amazing Portuegese hand-balancers, the Alexis Brothers, and the first Soviet act ever to perform independently in an American circus, the Panteleenko Brothers, who were authentic stars of the Russian circus (this was the beginning of the end for the Soviet regime). Katja Schumann, along with Carlos and Susanne Svenson (who would return to the Big Apple Circus 10 years later), provided the horsemanship — some of it quite hilarious thanks to the Svensons! An alumnus of the Big Apple Circus' Beyond the Ring® program, Carlos Guity, made his professional debut in this show.

All 1990 Photos: Patricia Lanza

Right: Olivier and Melinda Merlier. **Opposite page:** One of the last great ballerinas on horseback, Susanne Lind-Svenson.

107

Top left: Katja Schumann rides "en amazone" her American thoroughbred, Kha
Top right: Marie-Pierre Benac on the rotating trapeze. **Bottom left:** Vanessa Thomas.

Previous Pages: Left: The amazing Alexis Brothers. **Middle:** Gordoon on the rolling globe. **Right:** David Dimitri: one-arm stand on the tight wire.

Following Pages: Left: The Panteleenko Brothers. **Right:** Oaf in a delicate balancing exercise.

Top: Vanessa Thomas (the puppeteer), David Dimitri (Petrushka) and Marie-Pierre Benac. **Bottom:** Skye Williams with Ned

1991

Greetings from Coney Island

Conceived and directed by: **Paul Binder**

Musical Director: **Rik Albani**

Original Music: **Linda Hudes**

Clown Coordinator: **Michael Christensen**

Costumes by: **Donna Zakowska**

Lighting by: **Jan Kroeze**

Scenic design by: **James Leonard Joy**

Associate Director: **Dominique Jando**

Choreographer: **Lisa Giobbi**

Performance Directors: **Bryan Fox** & **Guy Manetti**

Cast: Dana Kaseeva - Katja Schumann - Olivier Merlier - Melinda Merlier - Les Frères Taquin - Marie-Pierre Benac - Elena Panova - Vanessa Thomas - The Rios Brothers - William Woodcock - The Flying Vazquez - Al Calienes - Yvonne Larson - **Ringmaster**: Paul Binder - **The Big Apple Circus Clowns**: Barry Lubin - Jeff Gordon - John Lepiarz - Taso Stavrakis

Among the old-timers of the Big Apple Circus's Creative Team, *Greetings From Coney Island* is still one of the favorites. It gathered an amazing constellation of circus stars: the inimitable and exciting hula-hoop act of the sensuous Dana Kaseeva (gold medalist at Paris's World Festival of the Circus of Tomorrow); the funny and moving pantomime of Les Frères Taquin (also gold medalists at the Paris festival); Russian solo-trapeze star Elena Panova (the third of the Paris festival gold medalists); the Rios Brothers (winners of the Silver Clown award at the International Circus Festival of Monte Carlo), returning by popular demand; and The Flying Vazquez (winners of the Gold Clown award in Monte Carlo), featuring the sensational quadruple somer-saulter Miguel Vazquez. Lisa Giobbi, a very talented choreographer joined the Creative Team.

All 1991 Photos: Patricia Lanza

Left: Olivier and Melinda Merlier.

Opposite page: The multi-talented cast of *Greetings from Coney Island*.

Top: Vanessa Thomas and the Woodcock Elephants. Left: The sensational Ri[os] Brothers. Opposite page: Certainly the greatest of all hula-hoop acts: the inim itable Dana Kaseeva.

Previous pages: Left page: Top: The undisputed queen of the swinging trapez[e] Elena Panova. Bottom left: Katja Schumann in an impressive exit. Bottom rig[ht:] The show's opening: Taso Stavrakis is the kid in the sailor suit, the lady is Ka[tja] Schumann, and Elena Panova plays the little girl. Right page: The wonderf[ul] Frères Taquin.

The Rios Brothers were international cabaret and circus stars. Their craft, risley, remains one of the most difficult genres to excel at. They were a great pleasure to work with.

P.B.

1992

Goin' Places

Conceived and directed by: **Paul Binder**
Music Director: **Rik Albani**
Original Music: **Linda Hudes**
Director of Clowning: **Michael Christensen**
Costume Design: **Donna Zakowska**
Lighting Design: **Jan Kroeze**
Scenic Design: **James Leonard Joy**
Associate Director: **Dominique Jando**
Choreographer: **Lisa Giobbi**
Performance Director: **Guillaume Dufresnoy**
Acrobatic Trainer: **Lucio Nicolodi**

Cast: Kristalleon ☆ Vanessa Thomas ☆ Vladimir Tsarkov ☆ César ☆ Johnny Peers ☆ Glen Nicolodi ☆ Julian Stachowski ☆ Melinda Merlier ☆ Marie-Pierre Benac ☆ Tunga ☆ The Egorov Troupe ☆ Katja Schumann ☆ Max Schumann ☆ Katherine Schumann Binder ☆ William Woodcock ☆ Yvonne Larson ☆ **Ringmaster**: Paul Binder ☆ **The Big Apple Circus Clowns**: Jeff Gordon, John Lepiarz, with Al Calienes

The working title of *Goin' Places* was *"The Wonderful Traveling Machine,"* referring to a machine that traveled not only to remote locations, but also into the dreams of the two clowns who manned it, Gordoon and Mr. Fish. The traveling machine itself, and many other scenic elements, were conceived by James Leonard Joy, who also experimented with an original set that changed its look according to the situation in the ring (it was to be used again in *Grandma Meets Mummenschanz*). The most dreamlike of all Big Apple Circus productions, it featured the clown-mime César, back by popular demand; Johnny Peers's hilarious Muttville Comix; the amazing juggler Vladimir Tsarkov; the extraordinary Mongolian contortionist Tunga; and the breathtaking mid-air maneuvers of the Egorov Troupe. The resident Company welcomed two new members, Glen Nicolodi (whose father, Lucio, had become the circus' acrobatic coach) and Julian Stachowski, who had come to the Circus with the Wozniak Troupe in 1985 and had stayed on in a managerial capacity when the troupe dissolved. The show also saw the acrobatic debut of Katherine Schumann Binder, the daughter of Paul Binder and Katja Schumann, and company member Vanessa Thomas made a strong impression dancing with Bill Woodcock's elephants.

All 1992 Photos: Theo O. Krath

Left: The amazing Tunga. **Opposite page:** Gordoon and Mr. Fish in the Traveling Machine, in front of James Leonard Joy's transforming set. The small figures in the ring were magically transformed into real performers during the opening.

Top: The spectacular aerial act of the Egorov Troupe. **Left:** Gordoon and Mr. Fish, the mad scientist, activate the magic garbage can... **Opposite page: Top:** The beautiful Tunga surrounded by the Spirit of the Air (Kristalleon) and the Spirit of the Earth (Vanessa Thomas). **Bottom:** The Undersea Tableau was performed in black light. Gordoon and Mr. Fish are sailing above, in the Traveling Machine.

Top left: Back by popular demand, César, and his invisible dog. Top right: The amazing juggler-contortionist Vladimir Tsarkov, the "Red Harlequin". Bottom left: Vanessa Thomas dancing with Anna May. Opposite page: Johnny Peers and his Muttville Comix.

Vanessa Thomas, on the elephant star Anna May, was breathtak-ingly beautiful.

P.B.

1993
Carnevale in Venice

Conceived and directed by: **Paul Binder**

Music Director: **Rik Albani**

Original Music: **Linda Hudes**

Director of Clowning: **Michael Christensen**

Costumes & Puppet Design: **Donna Zakowska**

Lighting Design: **Jan Kroeze**

Scenic Design: **James Leonard Joy**

Sound Design: **Judy Mareiniss**

Associate Director: **Dominique Jando**

Choreographer: **Lisa Giobbi**

Performance Director: **Guillaume Dufresnoy**

Acrobatic Trainer: **Lucio Nicolodi**

Assistant Performance Director: **Tom Larson**

Cast: Katja Schumann • Vanessa Thomas • John Lepiarz • Al Calienes • Melinda Merlier • Katherine Schumann Binder • Julian Stachowski • Vladimir Kobzar • Glen Nicolodi • Carlos Guity • James Clowney • Alfredo & Romano Colombaioni • Vesta Geschkova • Eli Milcheva • The Shenyang Acrobatic Troupe • The Collins Brothers • Max Schumann • Yvonne Larson • Max Binder • Serge Percelly • **Ringmaster**: Paul Binder

Thanks to the stunning costumes designed by Donna Zakowska and James Leonard Joy's superb scenic design, *Carnevale In Venice* is remembered as one of the most visually appealing of all Big Apple Circus shows. Italian clowns Alfredo & Romano Colombaioni gave it its specific flavor — although choreographer Lisa Giobbi and acrobatic trainer Lucio Nicolodi had significant input into the overall Italian atmosphere of the production! The highlights of the show were the charismatic Swiss juggler Serge Percelly, the Collins Brothers' uproarious comedy on the trapeze, and China's Shenyang Acrobatic Troupe in a spectacular aerial bungee act. Katja Schumann's superb equestrian presentation is also remembered as one the most inventive she ever staged. Two alumni of the Big Apple Circus' Beyond the Ring® program were now in the resident Company, Carlos Guity and James Clowney, where they were joined by new members Vesta Geschkova, Eli Milcheva, and Al Calienes.

All 1993 Photos: Theo O. Krath

Top: James Leonard Joy's superb set for Carnevale in Venice. **Right:** Katja Schumann and her father, Max Schumann. **Opposite page:** Donna Zakowska's magnificent costumes largely contributed to the success of *Carnevale in Venice*.

Top: Alfredo and Romano Colombaioni. **Left:** Melinda Merlier in the Pulchinella tableau. **Opposite page:** Top left: Max Schumann with his daughter's horses. **Top right:** James Clowney and Al Calienes (as Arlecchino) in the opening charivari. **Bottom left:** The charismatic juggler Serge Percelly. **Bottom right:** The Company in the opening charivari. Mr. Fish (Il Dottore) directs the traffic...

Previous pages:

Left: The hilarious Collins Brothers on the trapeze. **Right:** Glen Nicolodi. (No, he's not really balancing on his poodle's head!)

Following pages:

Left: The spectacular bungee act of the Shenyang Acrobatic Troupe. **Top right:** Beautiful Eli Milcheva and Vesta Geschkova brought Rhythmic Gymnastics to the ring. **Bottom:** The opening charivari: (l. to r.) Glen Nicolodi (in handstand), James Clowney, Carlos Guity, Al Calienes, Katherine Schumann Binder (running), John Lepiarz, Vladimir Kobzar, Julian Stachowski, Melinda Merlier (in handstand).

1994

Grandma Meets Mummenschanz

Conceived and directed by: **Paul Binder**

Music Director: **Rik Albani**

Original Music: **Linda Hudes**

Director of Clowning: **Michael Christensen**

Scenic Design: **James Leonard Joy**

Costume Design: **Donna Zakowska**

Lighting Design: **Jan Kroeze**

Sound Design: **Jim van Bergen**

Associate Director: **Dominique Jando**

Choreographer: **Lisa Giobbi**

Performance Director: **Guillaume Dufresnoy**

Acrobatic Trainer: **Lucio Nicolodi**

Assistant Performance Director: **Tom Larson**

Cast: Barry Lubin - Mummenschanz - Elena Panova - Darlene Williams - Skye & Stormy Williams - Ben Williams - Al Calienes - James Clowney - Vesta Geschkova - Carlos Guity - Yvonne Larson - Melinda Merlier - Eli Milcheva - Julian Stachowski - Katherine Schumann Binder - Vladimir Egorov - Jean Lemoine - Katja Schumann - Max Schumann - Lisa Dufresne - Max Binder - The Egorov Troupe - **Ringmaster**: Paul Binder

Grandma was back to meet the wonderful Swiss mime group, Mummenschanz. And so was the graceful Elena Panova — who, in addition to her amazing trapeze act, gave life to Mummenschanz's charming "flying clam." Jean Lemoine delighted Lincoln Center's audiences with his spinning plates (he was replaced on tour by a terrific juggler, Arturo Alegria, who would return a few seasons later), and the Egorov Troupe was back with its breathtaking aerial act. Max Binder made his trainer debut with a group of Indian Runner ducks — with some help from Lisa Dufresne.

All 1994 Photos: Theo O. Krath

Top: James Leonard Joy's *Goin' Places* transforming set was adapted and used once more for *Grandma Meets Mummenschanz*. **Right**: Jean Lemoine performed only at Lincoln Center, but was an audience favorite. **Opposite page**: A ticklish encounter between Grandma and one of Mummenschanz's giant hands.

Top: Katherine Schumann Binder's first balancing act, with Vladimir Egorov. Bottom: Max Binder first animal training act with a group of Indian Runner ducks. Opposite page, top: Grandma and Mummenschanz's "big mouth," which did a short trapeze act (known in the Circus as "the flying clam," it was animated by Elena Panova). Opposite page, bottom: Ben Williams tries to serve a meal to a facetious Anna May.

Previous pages:

Left: The beautiful "statue" act of James Clowney, Carlos Guity, and Melinda Merlier. Right: Elena Panova swinging on her trapeze, in her second appearance at the Big Apple Circus.

Max Binder is my son. He's been in the ring since the age of four, when he appeared as a crab in a blacklight seascape. One year he presented his dog, Scruffy; another year a group of Indian Runner ducks. He has assisted the clowns and the horse trainers and the ring crew. It has been a great way to bring up a kid with a sense of self-esteem and responsibility.

P.B.

1995

Jazzmatazz

Conceived and directed by: **Paul Binder**

Music Director: **Rik Albani**

Original Music: **Linda Hudes**

Director of Clowning: **Michael Christensen**

Scenic Design: **James Leonard Joy**

Costume Design: **David Belugou**

Lighting Design: **Jan Kroeze**

Sound Design: **Jim van Bergen**

Associate Director: **Dominique Jando**

Choreographer: **Lisa Giobbi**

Performance Director: **Guillaume Dufresnoy**

Acrobatic Trainer: **Lucio Nicolodi**

Company Act Consultant: **Guy Caron**

Assistant Performance Director: **Tom Larson**

Cast: Phil Stein ☆ Julian Stachowski ☆ Carlos Guity ☆ James Clowney ☆ Al Calienes ☆ Elena Panova ☆ Barry Lubin ☆ Katja Schumann ☆ Max Schumann ☆ Katherine Schumann Binder ☆ Elena Egorova ☆ Masha Dimitri ☆ Elizabeth Griffith ☆ The Rizhkov Trio ☆ Kris Kremo ☆ Melinda Merlier ☆ Max Binder ☆ Guillaume Dufresnoy/Tom Larson ☆ Vanessa Thomas ☆ The Egorov Troupe ☆ William Woodcock ☆ **Ringmaster**: Paul Binder

After the fantasy world of Mummenschanz, the Big Apple Circus returned to New York City, this time during the era of hot jazz and Prohibition. The legendary Swiss juggler Kris Kremo headed the cast, which featured Masha Dimitri on the slack-wire, the Rizhkov Trio on the trapeze, and the Egorov Troupe with their amazing Russian Barre act. And Katja Schumann jumped over a fully dressed dinner table with her high-school horse, Kahn. A new costume designer from Paris brought his talent to this production: David Belugou. The renowned Canadian director Guy Caron came on as a consultant — in preparation for his first directorial collaboration with the Big Apple Circus, two years later.

All 1995 Photos: Theo O. Krath

Left: Juggling star Kris Kremo. **Top:** The Rizhkov Trio: Their style led to the idea of *Jazzmatazz*. **Opposite page:** The spectacular Russian Barre act of the Egorov Troupe, with Regina Dobrovitskaya.

Top left: James Clowney, Al Calienes, and Elena Panova in the charivari.
Top right: Elena Egorova. **Left:** The cast of *Jazzmatazz*. **Above:** Technical design for the set by James Leonard Joy.

Opposite page: Top: Katja Schumann, riding Khan, jumps over the dinner table and the diners: Max Schumann, Lucio Nicolodi, Guillaume Dufresnoy, Melinda Merlier, and Tom Larson. **Bottom:** Masha Dimitri on the slack wire. On the left, a costume sketch by David Belugou.

1996

The Medicine Show

Conceived and directed by: **Paul Binder**

Music Director: **Rik Albani**

Original Music: **Linda Hudes**

Director of Clowning: **Michael Christensen**

Scenic Design: **Thomas Baker**

Costume Design: **David Belugou**

Lighting Design: **Jan Kroeze**

Sound Design: **Jim van Bergen**

Associate Director: **Dominique Jando**

Movement Director: **Masha Dimitri**

Performance Director: **Guillaume Dufresnoy**

Acrobatic Trainer: **Lucio Nicolodi**

Company Act Consultants: **Guy Caron, Michel Barette**

Assistant Performance Director: **Tom Larson**

Cast: Todd Robbins ☆ The Eskin Troupe ☆ James Clowney ☆ Carlos Guity ☆ Julian Stachowski ☆ Barry Lubin ☆ Johnny Peers ☆ Peggy O'Neill ☆ Greg DeSanto ☆ Sophie & Virgile ☆ Melinda Merlier ☆ William Woodcock ☆ Anatoli & Liubov Sudarchikovi ☆ Katja Schumann ☆ Max Schumann ☆ Max Binder ☆ Katherine Schumann Binder ☆ **Ringmaster:** Paul Binder

The *Medicine Show* was the last of the 19 productions directed by Artistic Director and Founder Paul Binder — and also one of the old-timers' favorites. The 1900s-era atmosphere was magnificently recreated by David Belugou's costumes. Todd Robbins, a Clown Care Unit® "Doctor of Delight," gave life to the fast-talking "Doc Pitchum". Johnny Peers and his Muttville Comix were back, and Greg DeSanto had joined Clown Alley. The highlights of the show were the spectacular (and funny) aerial bar act of the Eskin Troupe, the wonderful hand-to-hand balancing of Sophie & Virgile, and the mesmerizing costume transformations of Anatoli and Liubov Sudarchikovi. Bill Woodcock produced two superb elephant acts with company members Melinda Merlier and Carlos Guity. Michel Barette, who later directed several Big Apple Circus productions, consulted on Company acts with Guy Caron.

All 1996 Photos: Patricia Lanza

Top: Costume sketch by David Belugou. **Right:** Sophie & Virgile. **Opposite page:** Doc Pitchum (Todd Robbins), the Medicine Man, makes a triumphal entrance in the show opening.

Top: The dynamic rope jumping act of the Eskin Troupe, who doubled with a spectacular aerial bars act. **Left**: Grandma stuck between Happy (Greg DeSanto) and Doc Pitchum. **Opposite page**: Katja Schumann in a beautiful dress designed by David Belugou.

Previous pages:

Left: Anatoli and Liubov Sudarchikovi, mesmerizing quick-change artists. **Right**: The beautiful Melinda Merlier and the Woodcock Elephants.

1997

20 Years

Produced by: **Paul Binder**
Directed by: **Guy Caron** & **Michael Christensen**
Original Music: **Brigitte Larochelle**
Costume and Scenic Design: **David Belugou**
Lighting Design: **Sarah Sidman**
Choreography: **Gail Gilbert**
Sound Design: **Jim van Bergen**
Music Conductor: **Russell Johnson**
Acrobatic Trainer: **Lucio Nicolodi**
Performance Director: **Tom Larson**
Associate Artistic Director: **Dominique Jando**

Cast: Katja Schumann ✴ Barry Lubin ✴ Bello Nock ✴ William Woodcock ✴ Katherine Schumann Binder ✴ David Dimitri ✴ Regina Dobrovitskaya ✴ Carlos Guity ✴ Melinda Merlier ✴ Julian Stachowski ✴ Shannon Woodcock ✴ Elena Serafimovich ✴ The Flying Jimenez ✴ Max Binder ✴ Arturo Alegria ✴ The Kuznetsov Troupe

Guy Caron, the brilliant founder of Montreal's Ecole Nationale de Cirque and Cirque du Soleil's original artistic director, was the first guest director hired by the Big Apple Circus. He teamed up with the circus' Creative Director (and co-founder), Michael Christensen. This was indeed a special production, celebrating 20 years of success. But it was also a turning point, with the arrival of a talented new choreographer in Gail Gilbert, a new lighting designer named Sarah Sidman, and a new composer, the very creative Brigitte Larochelle. The entire production was beautifully designed by David Belugou. The performance, a remarkable piece of ensemble work, opened with a spectacular "elephants and acrobats" act created by Bill Woodcock and Lucio Nicolodi and involving the Big Apple Circus's resident Company. Alumnus David Dimitri was back for the occasion, and Bello Nock made his first appearance with the Big Apple Circus, on his way to becoming an audience favorite — and a true circus star. The beautiful Elena Serafimovich on the aerial ring, the amazing Kuznetsov Troupe on the Russian Barre, and the spectacular juggler Arturo Alegria also made unforgettable impressions. And multi-talented Regina Dobrovitskaya, formerly from the Egorov Troupe, joined the resident Company.

All 1997 Photos: Patricia Lanza

Left: A new "statue" act performed by Julian Stachowski, Regina Dobrovitskaya, Carlos Guity, and Melinda Merlier. **Opposite page:** The beautiful and amazing Elena Serafimovich on the aerial ring.

Top: Katja Schumann and her Arabian horses in the opening sequence.
Left: The finale tableau of *20 Years*. Opposite page, top: The triple somersault of Raul Jimenez. Bottom left: The dynamic juggler Arturo Alegria. Bottom right: The astounding Russian Barre act of the Kuznetsov Troupe.

Previous page:s

Left: Bello Nock, Anna May and William Woodcock. Right: David Dimitri returned to the Big Apple Circus for this 20th anniversary production.

1998

Happy On!

Produced by: **Paul Binder**

Directed by: **Guy Caron & Michael Christensen**

Composer/Music Coordinator: **Brigitte Larochelle**

Composer/Arranger: **Eddy Davis**

Costume Design: **David Belugou**

Scenic Design: **Dan Kuchar**

Lighting Design: **Sarah Sidman**

Choreography: **Gail Gilbert**

Sound Design: **Jim van Bergen**

Music Conductor: **Ugli Geissendoerfer**

Performance Director: **Tom Larson**

Associate Artistic Director: **Dominique Jando**

Acrobatic Trainer: **Vladimir Egorov**

Cast: Norman Barrett ⁕ Todd Robbins ⁕ The Liaoning Acrobatic Troupe ⁕ Julian Stachowski ⁕ Regina Dobrovitskaya ⁕ Ella Levitskaya ⁕ Bello Nock ⁕ Katja Schumann ⁕ Max Schumann ⁕ Max Binder ⁕ Molly Saudek ⁕ William & Shannon Woodcock ⁕ Song Hui Liadouze ⁕ Katherine Schumann Binder ⁕ The Kurziamovi ⁕ Mimi ⁕ Wang Lixin ⁕ **Ringmasters**: Paul Binder and Norman Barrett

The creative and directing team of Guy Caron and Michael Christensen was back for this wacky show, whose music was in large part inspired by Spike Jones. The People's Republic of China provided a large contingent of artists, and the Big Apple Circus invited the celebrated English ringmaster Norman Barrett to host the show and to delight the audiences with his hilarious budgie act. Molly Saudek on the tight wire and the aerial act of the Kurziamovi performing to Ravel's haunting "Bolero" were among the many highlights of this show, which confirmed the extraordinary appeal of Bello Nock. A new and extremely talented scenic designer, Dan Kuchar, joined the Creative Team.

All 1998 Photos: Bertrand Guay

Right: Bello Nock became a true star at the Big Apple Circus.
Opposite page: The Liaoning Acrobatic Troupe on the Chinese poles. Norman Barrett is in the background.

Previous pages:

Left: Balancing on a unicycle atop a rolling globe, Wang Lixin piles up on her head a series of bowls that she kicks up with her foot. **Right:** Ella Levitskaya and her performing bassets.

Top: The Liaoning Acrobatic Troupe's hoop divers. **Opposite page, top:** Katja Schumann and one of her Arabian stallions. **Bottom left:** Company members Regina Dobrovitskaya and Katherine Schumann Binder, with the Woodcock Elephants. **Bottom center:** The bungee act of the Liaoning Troupe. **Bottom right:** The amazing tight-wire dancer, Molly Saudek.

1999

Bello & Friends

Produced by: **Paul Binder**

Conceived by: **Michael Christensen**
& Michel Barrette

Directed by: **Michel Barette**

Original Music by: **Brigitte Larochelle**

Costume Design: **David Belugou**

Scenic Design: **Dan Kuchar**

Clowning Consultant: **Barry Lubin**

Choreographer: **Gail Gilbert**

Lighting Design: **Sarah Sidman**

Sound Design: **Thomas R. Wright**

Performance Director: **Tom Larson**

Music Director: **Russell Johnson**

Music Conductor: **Rob Slowik**

Associate Artistic Director: **Dominique Jando**

Acrobatic Trainer: **Vladimir Egorov**

Cast: Bello Nock ⁂ Francesco ⁂ Dinny McGuire ⁂ Violetta Ignatova ⁂ Julian Stachowski ⁂ Regina Dobrovitskaya ⁂ Katja Schumann ⁂ Sasha Nevidonski ⁂ Katherine Schumann Binder ⁂ The Jokers ⁂ Original Jugglers ⁂ Hernán ⁂ William & Shannon Woodcock ⁂ The Boichanovi **Ringmaster**: Paul Binder

Bello Nock was now an established star in his own right, and the show was built around his character. *Bello & Friends* was conceived by Michael Christensen and Canadian director Michel Barette, who was to direct this and two subsequent productions. It was a show rich in exceptional talent: the charming French musical clown Francesco; the wonderful dogs of Violetta Ignatova, who hailed from Russia; the Original Jugglers, also from Russia, and their spectacular "passing" act; the Jokers, perhaps the strongest classic flying act seen today; the charismatic Argentinian hand-balancer Hernán; and one of the all-time great teeterboard acts, the Boitchanovi, making its farewell appearance. Vladimir Egorov came aboard as Acrobatic Trainer and created an unique hand-to-hand balancing act for two gifted Company members, Julian Stachowski and Regina Dobrovitskaya. The talented new music conductor, Rob Slowik, was on his way to becoming the circus' new Musical Director

All *Bello & Friends'* Photos: Bertrand Guay

Top left: Dinny McGuire, the singing host. **Right**: The delightful Violetta Ignatova and her dogs. **Opposite page**: The star of the show, Bello Nock, in the opening sequence.

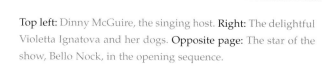

Previous pages:

Left page: The charismatic hand-balancer, Hernán.
Right page, top: The Jokers. Bottom: Julian
Stachowski and Regina Dobrovitskaya in an
original hand-to-hand balancing act created by
Vladimir Egorov.

These pages:

Top: The Original Jugglers. Left: The French clown Francesco. Right: The Medieval Tableau. Opposite
page, top: Katherine Schumann Binder and Sasha Nevidonski (on stilts), and Katja Schumann.
Bottom: Regina Dobrovitskaya and William Woodcock, with Ned and Anna May.

Following page:s Left: Ring Crew/Comedian Barney "Bo" Allen as Cupid. Right: Violetta Ignatova
with her Pomeranian dogs.

1999

Oops!
The Big Apple Circus Stage Show

Directed by: **Tony Walton**
Set Design: **Dan Kuchar**
Costume Design: **Tony Walton**
Lighting Design: **Brian Mason**
Choreographer: **Gail Gilbert**
Musical Arrangements: **Michael Amendola**
Sound Design: **Peter Fitzgerald**
Associate Costume Designer: **Rachel Gruer**
Associate Sound Designer: **Randy Hansen**
Assistant Lighting Designer: **Alexandra J. Pontone**
Musical Director: **Jeff Marder**
Production Coordinator: **Larry Sterner**
Artistic Associate: **Dominique Jando**

Scripted by Tony Walton and Michael Christensen - Based on a concept originally written, created and produced by Julie Greenberg and Jeff Jenkins as The Midnight Circus

Cast: Patricia Zasadny ❊ Alexandra Svirshch ❊ Norman Barrett ❊ Annette Devick ❊ Stephen Ringold ❊ The Kosakov Troupe ❊ Anna Kozakova ❊ Michael Lane Trautman ❊ Marijat Tabieva & Raouf Rasulov ❊ Paul Ponce ❊ Justin Case ❊ Vladimir & Olga Kurziamovi ❊ Don Otto ❊ The Lobanov Trio

The Big Apple Circus experimented for one season with a second unit, which performed on theater stages across the country. The show, whose concept fitted its theatrical format, was directed by Tony-, Oscar-, and Emmy-winning Broadway designer Tony Walton. This lavish and very funny show had an all-star cast headed by Norman Barrett (see *Happy On!*), and told the story of a Shakespearian theater company which unexpectedly had to share the stage with a circus troupe. Along with Norman, Stephen Ringold, Annette Devick, Justin Case, Michael Lane Trautman, and Don Otto dispensed large doses of comedy, while juggler Paul Ponce, aerialists Vladimir & Olga Kurziamovi and the Lobanov Trio, hand-balancers Rasulov & Tabieva, and the Kosakov troupe of acrobats provided thrills and excitement.

All *Oops'* Photos: Maike Schulz

Top: The cast of Oops!. **Right:** The amazing (and extremely funny) Justin Case. **Opposite page:** Stephen Ringold, as Richard III, prepares to cut Olga Lobanova in half, to the dismay of Annette Devick (as Ophelia) and Ringmaster Norman Barrett.

Previous page:s Top left: The Company in the show's final sequence. Bottom left: Michael Lane Trautman. Top right: Norman Barrett and his amazing trained budgies. Bottom right: The Kozakov Troupe provided several superb acrobatic acts to the show.

Left: High-speed juggler Paul Ponce. Above: Don Otto, the Diving Fool, caught in the diving board balustrade of his swimming pool/trampoline.

Above: The amazing hand-balancers Razulov & Tabieva.
Right: The spectacular aerial perch act of the Lobanovi twins.

Directing the strikingly international cast of Oops! *was amongst the most delicious experiences I've had the good fortune to enjoy in this naughty world of the entertainment business.*

Most of the non-English speaking performers had young children who picked up a smattering of English much quicker than their moms or dads. So many of my suggestions were filtered through these enchanting sprites — though sometimes it was hard for me to know whether what was being conveyed bore much resemblance to the direction I had attempted to give! Despite that, the process was a continual joy and delight.

Tony Walton

2000

Clown Around Town

Produced by: **Paul Binder**

Conceived and directed by: **Michael Christensen** &
Keith Anderson

Original Music by: **Brigitte Larochelle**

Costume Design: **David Belugou**

Scenic Design: **Dan Kuchar**

Director of Clowning: **Barry Lubin**

Musical Director: **Rob Slowik**

Choreographer: **Lisa LeAnn Dalton**

Lighting Design: **Christopher Gorzelnik**

Sound Design: **Thomas R. Wright**

Performance Director: **Tom Larson**

Associate Artistic Director: **Dominique Jando**

Acrobatic Trainer: **Vladimir Egorov**

Music Consultant: **Russell Johnson**

Creative Consultant: **Karen McCarty**

Cast: Jeff Gordon - Regina Dobrovitskaya ☼ Valdis Yanovskis ☼ Julian Stachowski ☼ Andrey Mantchev ☼ Nurgazy Nurken ☼ The Moroccan Connection ☼ Dinny McGuire ☼ Tom Dougherty ☼ Dania Kaseeva ☼ Mike & Pascale Sanger ☼ Katherine Schumann Binder ☼ Sasha Nevidonski ☼ Sophie & Virgile ☼ The Flying Pages ☼ Katja Schumann ☼ Max Binder ☼ Laura Schumann ☼ Serge Percelly ☼ The Slipchenko Trio ☼ David & Dania ☼ **Ringmaster**: Paul Binder

South Africa's very imaginative director Keith Anderson came aboard for this rich production, in which the City Clown (Gordoon, in a long overdue return appearance) got a visit from his Country Cousin, Orville (Tom Dougherty). A new choreographer, Lisa LeAnn Dalton, created an energetic opening charivari (with help from Vladimir Egorov) in which city "suits" turned flip-flaps and somersaults. Back by popular demand, the wonderful hand-balancers Sophie & Virgile and the dynamic Swiss juggler Serge Percelly were as successful as ever. Mike & Pascale Sanger delighted audiences with their apparently unruly dogs, while triple-somersaulter Jill Pages proved she was indeed one of the world's greatest female flyers. Company members Katherine Schumann Binder and Sasha Nevidonski created a beautiful aerial act on "silks" (known as a "tissu act"), but the talk of Clown Town was David and Dania (hula-hoopist Dana Kaseeva, last seen in *Greetings From Coney Island* in 1991) with their mind-boggling quick-change act.

All 2000 Photos: Bertrand Guay

Right: Jeff Gordon (Gordoon) made a long awaited comeback in *Clown Around Town*. **Opposite page:** The charming comedy dog act of Mike and Pascale Sanger.

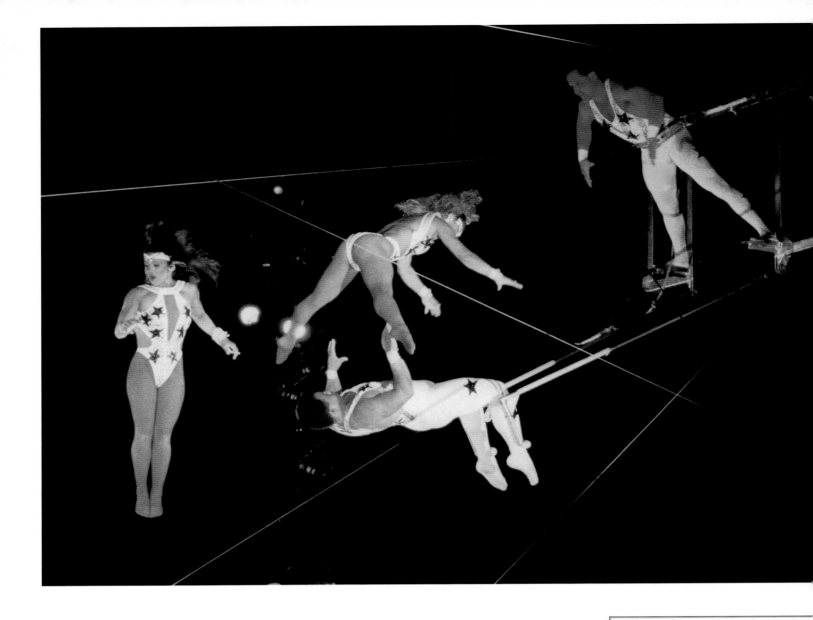

Above: The Flying Pages featured one of the greatest female flyers of all times, Jill Pages (on the left). Opposite page: Company members Katherine Schumann Binder and Sasha Nevidonski in their "silk act." The silhouette in the background is Regina Dobrovitskaya.

Previous pages

Left page: Top: Members of the Moroccan Connection played flipping baseball players. Bottom left: Dana Kaseeva and David Maas (David & Dania) stopped the show with their extraordinary quick-change act. Bottom Center: Serge Percelly made a much welcome come-back for this production. Bottom right: Gordoon during the finale of the show. Right page: Top: Cousin Orville (Tom Dougherty) plays with an audience member. Bottom: The opening charivari, with the "Wall Street tumblers." s

The Sudarchikovs and David & Dania each had quick-change acts that astounded our audience. People were constantly asking me, "How did she do that?" Since I wasn't sure, I was able to keep their secret.

Katherine Binder always seems to have a sense of pleasure about her performance. She's my daughter. We always said we would encourage her as an artist if that's what she wanted to do. Her joy makes supporting her work easy to do.

P.B.

2001

Big Top Doo-Wop

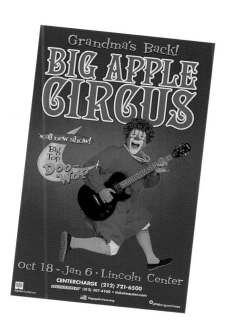

Produced by: **Paul Binder**
Conceived by: **Michael Christensen** &
Michel Barette
Directed by: **Michel Barette**
Original Music by: **Brigitte Larochelle**
Costume Design: **Mirena Rada**
Scenic Design: **Dan Kuchar**
Director of Clowning: **Barry Lubin**
Musical Director: **Rob Slowik**
Choreographer: **Lisa LeAnn Dalton**
Lighting Design: **Louis Morisset**
Sound Design: **Thomas R. Wright**
Performance Director: **Tom Larson**
Associate Artistic Director: **Dominique Jando**
Acrobatic Trainer: **Vladimir Egorov**
New Lyrics: **Ilene Weiss** &
Michael Christensen

Cast: Dinny McGuire   Dick Monday   Tiffany Riley   Maritza Atayde   Virgile Peyramaure   Andrey Mantchev   Christian Stoinev   Barry Lubin   The Olate Family   Katja Schumann   Katherine Schumann Binder   Max Binder   Sasha Nevidonski   Regina Dobrovitskaya   Valdis Yanovskis   Justin Case -   Carlos & Susanne Svenson - The Jokers   Emile Carey   The Maiorov Troupe   Mark Gindick

Canadian director Michel Barette was back for this tribute to the American Fifties. After a shaky start — its first dress-rehearsal was scheduled for September 11 — its very theme and spirit appeared as a welcome sign of unflappable continuity to New Yorkers. It also marked the long-awaited return of Grandma, Barry Lubin, after a three-year absence (Barry had served the show in other capacities during that time) assisted by his old partner from his Ringling days, Dick Monday , and the latter's equally talented wife, Tiffany Riley. The comedian-bicyclist Justin Case stopped the show. The production also revealed an extremely talented Canadian juggler, Emile Carey, and brought back the Jokers with their flying trapeze act and the equestrian comedy of Carlos and Susanne Svenson. A new costume designer made a brilliant circus debut with this production, Mirena Rada.

All 2001 Photos: Bertrand Guay

Opposite page: The finale of Big Top Doo-Wop, with the Maiorov Troupe in the center, Dinny McGuire on the Bandstand, Emile Carey on the left and Carlos Svenson on the right.

Top: The Olate family's rambunctious dogs can also be kept in line! Left: The show's opening: Emile Carey plays the guitar, while Sasha Nevidonski jumps over the group. Opposite page: The inimitable Justin Case

Knowing Michael Christensen and the Big Apple Circus, and being included in the work of the Clown Care Unit by spreading the word and creating new units all over the country, has been a great privilege for both myself and for my family.

When the children were little we went to the Big Apple Circus every chance we got. We continue to do so and only look forward to having grandchildren to bring there. The joy the Big Apple Circus gives our lives every year is just an indescribable gift.

Mandy Patinkin

Top left: The hilarious (and actually very difficult) equestrian act of the Svensons. Top right: Susanne Svenson, as the Lone Ranger, rides Katharina, the ostrich. Left: Grandma on her trcicyle. Opposite page: Dick Monday and Tiffany Riley (Slappy) in the show's opening.

Grandma has been an audience favorite for a long time. She's a little old lady who always manages to work her way into the ring and into our hearts.

P.B.

2002

Dreams of a City

Produced by: **Paul Binder**
Conceived by: **Michael Christensen** &
Michel Barette
Directed by: **Michel Barette**
Original Music by: **Scott Sena** & **Michael Valenti**
Costume Design: **Mirena Rada**
Scenic Design: **Dan Kuchar**
Director of Clowning: **Barry Lubin**
Musical Director: **Rob Slowik**
Choreographer: **Lisa LeAnn Dalton**
Lighting Design: **Louis Morisset**
Sound Design: **Darby Smotherman**
Performance Director: **Tom Larson**
Associate Artistic Director: **Dominique Jando**
Company Act Consultant: **Raffaele De Ritis**

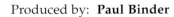

Cast: Barry Lubin ☆ Francesco ☆ Dinny McGuire ☆ Susanne Svenson ☆ Carlos Svenson ☆ Max Binder ☆ Regina Dobrovitskaya ☆ Valdis Yanovskis ☆ Andrey Mantchev ☆ Hans-Ludwig Suppmeier ☆ Michelle Youens ☆ Cong Tian ☆ The Aniskin Troupe ☆ Claudius Specht ☆ Katja Schumann ☆ Katherine Schumann Binder ☆ Sasha Nevidonski ☆ Irina Markova ☆ Uzeyir Novruzov ☆ Mark Gindick

And here it is, the Big Apple Circus' 25th production. Like the 10th anniversary show, *Dreams of a City* paid tribute to its roots in the classical equestrian circus of the nineteenth century. Inspired by the events of September 11, 2001 tragedy, however, it was also a tribute to the great spirit of New York, a city united in the very diversity of its immigrant population. The French clown Francesco, who had been featured with great success in *Bello & Friends*, was back, amidst a stellar cast that included the amazing Swiss juggler Claudius Specht; the spectacular flying act and trampoline acrobatics of the Russian Aniskin Troupe; from China, Cong Tian's unbelievable balancing feats on the slack wire (Silver Clown award at the Monte Carlo circus festival); the wonderful dogs of a great Russian trainer, Irina Markova; the energetic and charismatic balancer on free-standing ladder, Uzeyir Novruzov; and, of course, Grandma. The show's emphasis was put on traditional circus horsemanship, superbly provided by Katja Schumann, Katherine Schumann Binder, Max Binder, Susanne and Carlos Svenson, and a newcomer in the Company, Hans-Ludwig Suppmeier. Hans-Ludwig's wife Michelle Youens, along with Company alumni Regina Dobrovitskaya, Valdis Yanovskis, Andrey Mantchev, and Virgile Peyramaure appeared in various acts, on the ground and on horseback. Beautifully dressed by Dan Kuchar (set) and Mirena Rada (costumes), the show was once again directed by Michel Barette. Two new composers, Scott Sena and Michael Valenti, provided a splendid and colorful musical atmosphere.

All 2002 Photos: Bertrand Guay

Top left: Sketch for Katja Schumann's opening costume by Mirena Rada. **Top right:** Valdis Yanovskis at bottom, Virgile Peyramaure in the middle, and Regina Dobrovitskaya balancing at the top. The legs of Andrey Mantchev, who is perched on top of Valdis' head, appear from behind. **Left:** The amazing Claudius Specht juggles seven clubs — an extraordinary juggling feat.

Top: Grandma (Barry Lubin) and Francesco "at the beach." **Left:** The opening tableau: Carlos Svenson leads the "immigrants." **Opposite page:** Top left: Michelle Youens and Katherine Schumann Binder with Dinny McGuire, "The Man Who Robbed the Bank in Monte-Carlo." **Bottom left:** Katherine Schumann Binder, Regina Dobrovitskaya, Michelle Youens and the cast in the opening sequence.

Previous pages:

Left: The energetic Azerbaijani balancer on free-standing ladders: Uzeyir Novruzov. **Right:** The pyramid on horseback: (l. to r.) Hans-Ludwig Suppmeier, Michelle Youens, Valdis Yanovskis, Regina Dobrovitskaya, Carlos Svenson, and Andrey Mantchev.

Following pages:

Left:
Right: The incredible balancer on the slack wire, Cong Tian.

Pages 198, 199

Left: The spectacular Aniskin Troupe in full flight.
Right: Katja Schumann in an original presentation involving horses and… "tissus".

ℬehind the Curtain

The first time Paul Binder and Michael Christensen stepped into the ring of the Nouveau Cirque de Paris, they sensed the special feeling that the circus bestows on performers and audience members alike. Everything is possible in the circus: One can fly, share space and time with wild animals, and achieve extraordinary feats of strength and agility — and all without the help of computerized effects! You leave with a feeling of exhilaration, of joy through achievement. When Paul and Michael founded the Big Apple Circus, they wanted to share this unique sense of renewal with the communities the circus would serve, to connect people with their positive emotions — both in and outside the ring. Today, behind the curtain, the Big Apple Circus continues that commitment through four major community outreach programs that are nearly as renowned as the circus itself.

Beyond the Ring

As we have seen earlier, what is officially known today as the Big Apple Circus, Ltd. was originally founded as the New York School for Circus Arts, Inc. The Big Apple Circus was, in effect, its performing arm, and the school's students formed the core of the first Big Apple Circus productions. By 1983, however, the organization had reached a financial crossroads, and its directors realized it could not support both a professional circus school and the circus itself, which was beginning to attract international circus stars. Rather than fold the school, it was decided to fully convert the school it into one of the roles it already played. The New York School for Circus Arts thus became the Big Apple Circus's first full-fledged community outreach program, Beyond the Ring®.

Today, this educational program operates in-school and after-school programs in New York City public schools, primarily in districts facing fiscal challenges, often without physical education programs. By teaching circus arts — and circus values — to the children in these schools, Beyond the Ring not only provides a valuable cultural and educational resource, it also helps children build self-esteem and appreciate the value of teamwork. Among the skills taught are juggling, clowning, unicycle, stilt-walking, tumbling, acrobatics, and aerial gymnastics. Stars of the Big Apple Circus's professional shows are often guest lecturers. At the end of each program, Beyond the Ring students put on a gala circus show for their schoolmates, parents, and friends. The best of them become part of the Expert Student Troupe which performs at festivals and special events and also helps teach the classes. They too discover the amazing powers of the human spirit through circus arts.

Above: Students of the Beyond the Ring® program put on a show for their peers and families.

Circus for All

Back in 1977, Con Edison granted the Big Apple Circus a subsidy to give free tickets to youths from New York City's poorest neighborhoods. That generosity not only was a godsend to the circus's shoestring finances, it also brought into the tent some of the Big Apple Circus' most excited and enthusiastic audiences. Today, the Big Apple

Photo: Robb D. Cohen

Above: A child touches Dinny McGuire's moustache at a Circus of the Senses® performance. Below: After the show, Circus of the Senses« audiences are invited in the ring to discover the animal performers they couldn't see.

Photo: Christopher Little

It is rare that the needs of our blind and visually impaired consumers are so thoroughly addressed in what is considered a "mostly visual" experience. The narration provided, via head sets as well as the Braille and large-type programs, enabled our consumers to follow and enjoy the program. Because of these adaptations, the blind person was informed prior to the act what was about to happen. For a blind parent or child, this was especially rewarding. For the first time, everyone in the family could enjoy a performance together.

Nancy D. Miller
Executive Director
VISIONS / Services for the Blind and
Visually Impaired

Circus itself has for years been wholly self-supporting, but its tradition of giving subsidized tickets continues unabated. Operating through its Circus For All® program, the Big Apple Circus now distributes nearly 50,000 complimentary or discounted tickets per year to organizations serving disadvantaged children. This enables economically and physically challenged children to experience the excitement and wonder of the circus. For many, this is also their first experience of a live theatrical performance.

Circus of the Senses

The Big Apple Circus's community outreach programs are guided by a tradition of being accessible to as broad and diverse an audience as possible. No program is more attuned to this idea than Circus of the Senses®, which was developed in 1988 with the support of the Butler Foundation. Circus of the Senses is a special circus performance designed to meet the demands of children with sight and hearing impairments and other special needs. Using Braille and large-type programs, American Sign Language interpreters, and infrared headsets giving "play-by-play" description of the action in the ring, this audience is able to enjoy the circus show, almost all for the first time. This unique experience also includes a post-performance "touch session" in the ring, where blind children are able to meet and interact with some of the human and animal performers.

Recently, thanks to the generosity of JPMorgan Chase and the Hasbro Children's Foundation, the Big Apple Circus has been able to offer Circus of the Senses performances in Atlanta, Boston, Somerset, NJ, and Washington, DC — in addition to these annually held in New York City. Each year, 8,000 to 10,000 guests are able to enjoy these truly extraordinary performances.

The Clown Care Unit

The premier community outreach program of the Big Apple Circus is the now world-famous Clown Care Unit®. This effort began in 1986, when Michael Christensen, then still performing in the ring as Mr. Stubs, was invited to entertain young patients at New York City's Babies and Children's Hospital. But let us hear Michael himself tell the story:

> In the late summer of 1985, doctors diagnosed my brother Kenneth with pancreatic cancer and gave him four months to live. He died two months later. He was 42 years old. Before he died, he presented me with a doctor's bag he had picked up at a flea market for $3.50: "You're a clown, Michael. Maybe you can use it."

> In the spring of the following year, as I sat at my desk in the old administrative offices of the Big Apple Circus at 104th Street and Fifth Avenue, I answered a call: *"Are you Michael Christensen?" … "Yes, I am." … "My name is Virginia Keim, Chief Officer of Development of Babies Hospital at Columbia Presbyterian Medical Center, and I've been secretly I love with you for years."* She got my attention. She continued: *"Babies Hospital is a heart-transplant specialty facility, and every two years we host an event called Heart Day. All the children who've had heart surgery,*

their families, and the medical and administrative staffs get together to celebrate the simple fact they are alive! I would like to invite you to perform for them." I said I would, and I recruited two other clowns from the Big Apple Circus, Barry Lubin, who is "Grandma," and Jeff Gordon, better known as "Gordoon," to join me. We instantly became, Dr. Stubs, Chief Dietician Grandma, and Disorderly Gordoon.

In that spring of 1986, as Dr. Stubs, I strode across the stage to the podium of Alumni Auditorium at Columbia Presbyterian Medical Center in New York City, and announced: "I'm taking over!" And for the next 20 minutes, along with my clownical colleagues, we did just that! Chief Dietician Grandma demonstrated popcorn-eating techniques. Disorderly Gordoon showed everyone how to dispense an entire roll of toilet paper into the air using a leaf blower. We had heart surgeons assist us in goofy hearing tests, eye tests, and at one point we donned cat masks and took the guesswork out of cat scans. I concluded by having a young heart-transplant patient perform a red nose transplant on her some-what nervous, but still game, surgeon.

We had a ball! It was the most fulfilling twenty minutes of my professional career. And what was I holding in my hand? The medical bag, a most precious gift from my brother Kenneth. Little did I realize the tattered doctor's bag, Heart Day, and those wonderfully insane 20 minutes would lead to the creation of the Big Apple Circus Clown Care Unit.

Photo: Kathy A Weydig

Above: Clown Doctor at work: Liz Bolick (Dr Sneakers).

During those 20 magical minutes, Michael experienced the extraordinary power of laughter. Many hospital patients feel afraid, and children most of all. These feelings are only intensified by the hospital's atmosphere of seriousness and tension. But when a clown donning a white medical coat unexpectedly takes the place of the doc-tor — the symbol of power and authority, the ringmaster of the hospital ward — the tension and fear associated with his image vanish. Everything returns to a human dimension — as it does in the circus when a clown parodies an acrobat, or, for that matter, when a clown makes fun of the ringmaster. During those 20 magical minutes, Michael sensed the need for children in a hospital to still be part of a world filled with joy and laughter. Once, in a hospital elevator, a grumpy doctor told Dr. Stubs: "Clowns don't belong in the Intensive Care Unit." Dr. Stubs replied, "Neither do children."

In 1987, with a grant from the Altman Foundation, a very silly yet very worthy group of "clown doctors" began to make "clown rounds" in some of the New York City's leading pediatric hospitals — the Clown Care Unit. They did what clowns do best: bring laughter where it is least expected and therefore most needed. In 1996, in response to growing demand for its services, the Big Apple Circus Clown Care Unit launched a national expansion plan beginning at Children's Hospital Boston. Its goals were to establish new programs in nationally ranked pediatric facilities serving the largest and most diverse populations of seriously ill children.

Today, more than 90 clown doctors — professional performers specially selected and trained to work in the sensitive hospital environment — conduct clown rounds three to five days a week year round at the bedsides of acutely and chronically ill or injured children. The Clown Care Unit now operates in 17 hospitals in New York City (seven facilities), Atlanta, Baltimore, Boston, Chicago, Miami, New Haven, Seattle, and Washington, D.C., and its clown doctors make over 200,000 bedside visits annually. It also collaborates with partner programs, all created by Clown Care Unit alumni, in France, Germany, Brazil, and Italy.

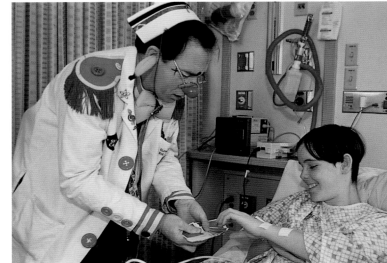

Kim, "Dr. Loon," played his concertina for the young boy. The boy's eyes widened, his face glowed. Later a doctor told Kim that surgeons had just restored the boy's hearing and this was the first music he had ever heard.

Michael Christensen

We were playing with a young girl about seven years old and recovering from a brain operation. Sometimes, I've learned, after these operations the facial muscles cannot be controlled for a while after the procedure. BB and I were up to our usual nonsense when the young girl broke into an incredible smile. Now here was the kicker: Dad jumped up and said excitedly, "You brought back her dimples" Apparently, when she first started smiling after she woke up, her parents noticed that she didn't have her dimples anymore. But after one session with clown specialists, BAM! — dimples. Dad was so excited that he went and got his wife from the hallway to show her the renewed dimples. I love my job.

Dr. Gonzo and Nurse BB,
Children's Hospital, Boston

In Cardiac Step-Down we had a joyous and touching experience. A baby, recently out of heart surgery, wide awake and alone, responded to our music and songs by tapping his foot, literally in rhythm with the bouncy beat of the song. He stared at us with the wildest eyes imaginable and just kept on tapping that foot. He stopped when we stopped, so we started again, and that foot went on a-tapping, telling us how this child was responding to our sounds.

Judy Gail (Dr. La La La Loca)
Miami Children's Hospital

We knew his days were numbered, and he had both accepted and rejected us in the past. He was 14 years old and spoke a little more English than his parents. When we entered his room was dark and he was lying on the bed with his eyes closed. All around the room people were sitting, all very somber, dark and quiet. Mom sat quietly on the far side of the room and smiled as we came in. We took that as a "Yes, come play." We gently shut the door behind us and then I ran across the room and said "Mamma!" giving her a big hug in the process. Everyone laughed. I hugged the person next to her and more laughter erupted. At the end of the routine the whole family was laughing, and our friend in bed was wearing a red nose and smiling and beautiful.

Dr. Bonky and Dr. Grizelda Lefou,
Children's Hospital & Regional Medical Center, Seattle

The first thing I noticed is how freaked out this little girl looked. It was as if she had fallen asleep safe and sound and woke up in the hospital with all this gear on her. Her father had this intense look about him, like silent screaming. However, there was something else too . It was a glimmer of "Please, make my child normal, please." BB and I worked sooo cautiously, playing soft music, using a hand beeper to make her stuffed animals squeak and using hand coils to decorate her room. Then she giggled. It felt like we had all been struck by lightning. We all stood there, wondering if we had really heard it or if it was our imagination, when she did it again. Dad now had fireworks going off his eyes. He was so excited.

Rob Preskins (Dr. Gonzo)
Children's Hospital, Boston

We met the Chinese family in the Intensive Care Unit. Their baby was very ill. The mood was intense; I tipped my hat and passed by. The next day, the baby was better and the mood lightened, so we blew some bubbles and played music. The baby's health improved and doctors transferred him to a regular in-patient service floor. We got really silly with this family for the next several visits. Finally, we paraded them down the corridors, through the hallways, out the doors and waved goodbye. We never knew their names, spoke their language or knew what was wrong. We didn't need to.

Michael Christensen

The Chief of Pediatric Emergency Department came to follow-up on a child. "C" was very withdrawn and would not speak to anyone. The doctor and several residents stopped as they left the room and told the nurses, the child life specialist and us clowns: "I prescribe large doses of clown for this young lady!" We obliged with a visit. Dr. Short and I (Dr. Boots) threw everything we had at her! (Not literally) We had no luck and no laughs. The child life specialist mentioned that C might not be able to see our silly shoes. Dr. Short lifted his legs one at a time to display his oversized tennis shoes. I responded by displaying a stocking clad foot minus the shoe. The shoe was instead on my hand. Dr. Short bending over to investigate presented me with a huge target. I bopped him on the butt with my oversized shoe. C answered with a laugh and smiled slightly. We continued this line of performing and ended up with C erupting in genuine laughter. We left and the child life specialist was able to follow-up and engage C further. Truly a team effort!

Dr. Boots and Dr. Short,
Johns Hopkins Children's Center

Above: The "Doctors of Delight" doing what they do best: **Top left:** Joe Barney (Doc Geezer) and Liz Bolick (Dr. Sneakers). **Top right:** Nurse B.B. (Bob Widdop). **Opposite page, left:** Kim Winslow (Dr. Loon) **Opposite page, right:** Bob Widdop (Nurse B.B.)

The therapist had been working unsuccessfully with the girl for 20 minutes trying to get her to move her tongue. Nothing seemed to work. I looked at Laine, "Dr. EBDBD." She looked at me. We both childishly stuck out our tongues at the therapist. The child laughed and stuck out her tongue as well. The therapist gasped.

Michael Christensen

Credits

Editor-in-Chief: Dominique Jando
Managing Editor: Jim Roper
Book Design: Anne Lawrence

Line Editor: Andrew Coe
Contributing Writers: Don Covington, Paul Cothran

Illustrations from the Big Apple Circus Archive.
Principal photography by Bertrand Guay, Jean-Marie Guyaux,
Theo O. Krath, Patricia Lanza, Lynn Saville, Maike Schulz
(The photography for the Big Apple Circus's first season by Peter Angelo Simon)

Published by Big Apple Circus, Ltd.
in association with Odyssey Publications
Distributed in the United States by W. W. Norton

Produced and printed by Twin Age Limited, Hong Kong
Printed in China

Acknowledgments

We wish to extend our heartfelt thanks to the heroes of this book, Paul Binder and Michael Christensen, for sharing their memories of their European adventures and of the Big Apple Circus's struggling early days — and mostly for having conceived the Big Apple Circus! At the Big Apple Circus, our thanks also go to Gary Dunning, Executive Director, and Thomas Martin, Chief Financial Officer, for their support. And for all sorts of help, we thank Joel Dein, Director of Communications, Paul Cothran, Director of Health and Community Programs, Thomas M. Exton, Director of Development, Laura Wingate, Karen McCarty, Danielle Giorgetti, the "Doctors of Delight" at the Clown Care Unit®, Jennifer Thorpe, and practically everyone else. On the "lot," we must give special mention to Don Covington, Michael LeClaire, Jim (Jimbo) Page, Karen Scott, Anne Covington, Katherine Schumann Binder, and of course Barry (Grandma) Lubin, whose image graces the cover of this book (he's the little lady in red, not the grey butterfly with a trunk). We also express our gratitude to Margaret Tanzosh and Jeff Williamson, at Avenue C Productions, who first studied the feasibility of this project; Magnus Bartlett, at Airphoto International, who turned it into a reality; Andrew Coe, our editor, who reminded us constantly that what is obvious to us is not necessarily so to the reader, and therefore asked plenty of questions; Anne Lawrence, who showed taste and patience in choosing among the hundreds of documents we dropped on her lap, and great talent in designing a truly beautiful book. We also salute our extremely talented show photographers, who so wonderfully chronicled the Big Apple Circus over these 25 years: Jean-Marie Guyaux, Lynn Saville, Linda Rivero, Linda Alaniz for Martha Swope, and especially Patricia Lanza, Theo O. Krath, Maike Schulz, and Bertrand Guay — with special thanks to Peter Angelo Simon, the Big Apple Circus's very first chronicler. The Big Apple Circus wishes to thank all the above and any other photographer whose work has been included but inadvertently not been appropriately credited. Finally, we thank the numerous circus artists whose names and/or pictures appear in the pages of this book, and who have graced the ring of the Big Apple Circus: their amazing talent not only made the Big Apple Circus what it is, but it made the lives of those who saw them richer. This book is dedicated to them, and to everyone who participated, at one time or another, in the great adventure of the Big Apple Circus.

(Photo: see p. 179)

Dominique Jando and Jim Roper

Big Apple Circus – 25 Years

First edition 2003 © Big Apple Circus Ltd.

Published by Big Apple Circus, Ltd.
505 Eighth Avenue, New York, NY 10018
Web: www.bigapplecircus.org
in association with Odyssey Guides,
an imprint of Airphoto International Ltd.
Web: www.odysseypublications.com

Airphoto International Ltd., 1401 Chung Ying Building,
20–20A Connaught Road West, Sheung Wan, Hong Kong
Tel: (852) 2856 3896; Fax: (852) 2565 8004; E-mail: odysseyb@netvigator.com

Twin AgeLimited, Hong Kong. E-mail: twinage@netvigator.com

Printed in China

ISBN: 962-217-723-9 (hardback)
ISBN: 962-217-724-7 (paperback)

Distributed in the United States of America by
W.W. Norton & Company, Inc.,
500 Fifth Avenue, New York, NY 10110
Tel: 800-233-4830
Web: www.wwnorton.com

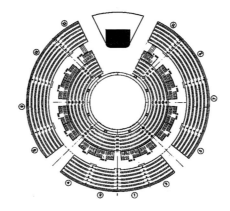